T0329301

Cambridge Elements ☰

Elements in Shakespeare Performance
edited by
W. B. Worthen
Barnard College

SHAKESPEARE, BLACKFACE AND RACE

Different Perspectives

Coen Heijes
University of Groningen

CAMBRIDGE
UNIVERSITY PRESS

CAMBRIDGE
UNIVERSITY PRESS

University Printing House, Cambridge CB2 8BS, United Kingdom

One Liberty Plaza, 20th Floor, New York, NY 10006, USA

477 Williamstown Road, Port Melbourne, VIC 3207, Australia

314–321, 3rd Floor, Plot 3, Splendor Forum, Jasola District Centre,
New Delhi – 110025, India

79 Anson Road, #06–04/06, Singapore 079906

Cambridge University Press is part of the University of Cambridge.

It furthers the University's mission by disseminating knowledge in the pursuit of
education, learning, and research at the highest international levels of excellence.

www.cambridge.org
Information on this title: www.cambridge.org/9781108827829
DOI: 10.1017/9781108900546

First published 2020

A catalogue record for this publication is available from the British Library.

ISBN 978-1-108-82782-9 Paperback
ISSN 2516-0117 (online)
ISSN 2516-0109 (print)

Shakespeare, Blackface and Race

Different Perspectives

Elements in Shakespeare Performance

DOI: 10.1017/9781108900546

First published online: September 2020

Coen Heijes

University of Groningen

Author for correspondence: Coen Heijes, c.p.a.heijes@rug.nl

ABSTRACT: This Element addresses the topical debate on blackface, race and Othello. With Shakespeare performance studies being rather Anglo-centric, the author explores how this debate has taken a radically different course in the Netherlands, a country historically perceived as tolerant and culturally close to the UK. Through several case studies, including the Van Hove Othello of 2003/2012 and the latest, controversial 2018/2020 Othello, the first main house production with a black actor as Othello, the author analyses the interaction between blackface and (institutional) racism in Dutch society and theatre and how Othello has become an active player in this debate.

KEYWORDS: Othello, blackface, race, performance, Shakespeare

ISBNs: 9781108827829 (PB), 9781108900546 (OC)

ISSNs: 2516-0117 (online), 2516-0109 (print)

Contents

1 Introduction

In December 2019, the annual worldwide controversy regarding the Dutch character Black Pete (an extremely popular tradition among kids, in which white adults blacken their faces) broke out once again, attracting more critical attention than ever before. Various news outlets such as the *Guardian*, the *Independent*, the *New York Times*, the *Los Angeles Times*, the *Indian Express*, *Frankfurter Allgemeine*, BBC, CNN and Al Jazeera, to name a few, highlighted the ongoing debate on blackface traditions, and celebrities such as Kim Kardashian, Trey Songz and American rapper Waka Flocka Flame weighed in on the debate, speaking out against the tradition. In 2018, a Dutch *Othello* production by Daria Bukvić also entered this controversy and challenged Dutch blackface traditions and institutional racism in Dutch society. Interestingly, this was also the first main house production in the Netherlands wherein Othello was played by a black person. While the use of blackface in *Othello* has long been discredited in anglophone countries, this has not been the case in many other countries, although mainstream Shakespeare criticism conveys, at times, a somewhat unquestioning acceptance that blackface condemnation represents a global phenomenon. With Shakespeare performance studies being Anglo-centric, the scholarly community is often ignorant of case studies that examine the interaction of institutional racism, society, blackface traditions and history and how these interact with *Othello* productions. In this study, the author takes a different approach to blackface in *Othello* in a country which is, out of all EU countries, probably politically and culturally the closest to the UK and is also historically perceived as a tolerant country. As such, this Element analyses not only the Dutch tradition of blackface in *Othello*, but also how this responded to and even supported a possible paradox in society: the coexistence of institutional racism and xenophobia alongside the (self-)perception of a tolerant society and denial of racial discrimination.

1.1 The Demise of Blackface in Othello

An overwhelming majority of research on *Othello* and blackface is based on the situation in anglophone countries, with the UK and the USA being the most researched countries. The consensus is that up to the 1960s, mainly white actors would play Othello in movie and theatre productions, while the use of blackface seemed to be standard practice in most instances. In general studies and sourcebooks on *Othello* or Shakespeare and race, there is an almost paradigmatic group of examples for this tradition used repeatedly in illustrating the performance history of theatre and movie productions of the play (e.g. Alexander & Wells, 2000; Hadfield, 2003; Hankey, 2005; Jarrett-Macauley, 2017; Kolin, 2002; Neill, 2006; Potter, 2002; Thompson, 2006, 2016; Vaughan, 1994; Vaughan & Cartwright, 1991). These works invariably include a group of early black actors, such as Ira Aldridge and Paul Robeson, who at the time were a minority in a predominantly white actor environment for the role. Likewise, post-war blackface performances by white actors such as Laurence Olivier and Orson Welles are also generally included in these studies. While in the UK, the reaction to Olivier's Othello in the mid-1960s was overall positive, the US reception expressed far more discomfort.

From the 1960s onwards, a gradual decline can be seen in the use of blackface, often explained by factors such as the increase in awareness about race, the civil rights movement, unwanted associations with minstrel shows and growing racial tensions in society. Although blackface continued into the 1980s in the UK, lighter make-up than before was being applied. The 1981 *Othello*, with Anthony Hopkins as Othello in the BBC Shakespeare Series, is often considered a turning point in the British tradition after an outcry over the casting decision and the refusal to address racial issues (Potter, 2002: 154–6). Both in the USA and in the UK, white actors retreated from the role, the use of blackface was increasingly discredited, and a consensus developed that only actors of colour could play the role thereon (Thompson, 2016: 83). Looking back on the *Othello* with Laurence Olivier, Rozett (1991: 265) mentioned how she wished that she had not shown the movie to her students and described Olivier's depiction of Othello as 'dated – one cannot imagine a white, prominent actor employing such exaggerated blackface makeup today'. While arguably true of the Shakespeare tradition in the UK and the USA, the remark also highlighted the discrepancy between these developments and those in many other countries at the time.

At the end of the twentieth century and during the twenty-first, tensions in the Middle East, the effects of 9/11 and the ongoing wars in Afghanistan and Iraq also found their way into *Othello*. More military-oriented productions, a focus on Othello's Arab roots, the relation to tensions with Muslims and the psychological effects of war on soldiers became increasingly important themes in productions of the play. Recent prominent examples include Nicholas Hytner's production in the National Theatre (2013), Ron Daniels' Shakespeare Theatre Company's *Othello* (2016) and Richard Twyman and Abdul Rahman-Malik's *Othello* in the Tobacco Factory (2017). While these productions presented Othello above all as a man rather than as a representative of a specific country or race, he was positioned as a Muslim and a military man. Although the racial topic became less central in these productions, the use of blackface or white actors without blackface for the title role in *Othello* had practically disappeared by this time, with some notable exceptions, in which case these choices were inevitably a prominent topic of debate in reviews and academic research. A constantly recurring example in performance research to illustrate this point was Jude Kelly's 1997 Shakespeare Theatre *Othello* with Patrick Stewart as Othello, surrounded by an almost entirely black cast (Hankey, 2005: 107–11; Iyengar, 2002: 118–24; Potter, 2002: 179–84).

The same year, the performance of young black actor David Harewood as Othello at the National Theatre led to a discussion in British media about the reluctance in casting white actors as Othello, which some considered reverse discrimination (Neill, 2006: 65; Wheatcroft, 1997). In the debate on race and casting in Othello, actor Hugh Quarshie and playwright Kwame Kwei-Armah raised the topic of whether black actors should consider if it is ethical at all to play Othello, arguing that it might risk reinforcing the racial stereotypes that pervade the play (Quarshie, 1999; Kwei-Armah, 2004). Further, almost two decades after David Harewood's performance, actor and director Steven Berkoff and Shakespeare scholar Stanley Wells urged the theatre industry to 'grow up' and allow white actors to play such roles (Berkoff, 2015; Wells, 2015). However, despite these discussions, white actors are still a rarity for this role and inevitably invite comments, while the use of blackface itself seems to be a thing of the past in *Othello* productions on the main anglophone stage. As blackface recently also started to disappear from the operatic *Otello*, with Latvian tenor Aleksandrs Antonenko abandoning the practice in the 2015 Metropolitan Opera production, reviewers reported that the change came more 'than a generation after leading theatre companies stopped "blacking up" white actors to play

Othello in Shakespeare's play' (Cooper, 2015). While this is true of the tradition in many anglophone countries, the perspective might have been less valid for other parts of the world.

1.2 Non-anglophone Othello

While much could be said about the dichotomy between anglophone and non-anglophone Shakespeare, it is a differentiation which is commonly made when comparing *Othello* productions around the world. Although most attention has focused on the USA and the UK, so-called global Shakespeare, also known by many other terms, has increased interest in and study of *Othello* in other countries. However, casting decisions and the use of blackface are in many countries still relatively unexplored. Kolin (2002: 53–8) pointed out how in non-Western countries the signifiers for race were different, how the importance of 'Otherness' gained a new meaning, and how the specific theatrical and political conditions influenced productions. Loomba (2008: 129–36) indicated how racial politics could be completely erased from the play in India or how *Othello* could also be used to address racism in India. Potter (2002: 174–9) argued that the involvement in the slave trade would have caused productions of *Othello* in the USA and the UK to be 'always more tinged with unease than those in the rest of the world', although also providing examples of how a Japanese, German and South African production of *Othello* responded in different ways to national racial discourses. Likewise, Thompson (2016: 97–102) included a South African, a German and a Singaporean *Othello* in her production overview of the play, and Hankey (2005: 93–7) included a production from South Africa. The 1990 South African *Othello* by Janet Suzman, directed at the Market Theatre in Johannesburg, has by now turned into another example which has entered the 'performance canon' and is unfailingly discussed in overviews. Apart from its content, her use of the English language, the entanglement of British and South African history, the close relation with the British theatre world and its ready accessibility might have added to its prominence.

While the anglophone and semi-anglophone productions referred to in the research on *Othello*, race, blackface and casting tend to employ a rather standard and almost paradigmatic set of productions, non-anglophone examples demonstrate a wider variety, although there has been a tendency to focus on non-Western countries in Asia and Africa in research, also due to their supposedly larger difference with the USA and the UK for their role in the slave trade and the ensuing racial discourse and demographic composition (Kolin, 2002; Potter, 2002). In the non-anglophone, Western context of *Othello*, race and blackface, a limited number of German productions received a lot of attention in literature. These were mainly the more controversial productions, such as Peter Zadek's 1976 *Othello*, which caricatured and deconstructed racial stereotypes (Hankey, 2005: 85; Kennedy, 1996: 269–70), or the 2006 *Othello* by Luk Perceval, who combined the racial agenda with the casting of a white Othello (Billing, 2007). Other controversial German productions that used a white Othello were Jette Steckel's Deutsches Theater Berlin *Othello* (2009), which challenged racial and gender stereotypes and featured an Othello played by a white, female actress dressed in a gorilla costume, and the 2011 *Othello* by Thomas Ostermeier, whose choice of a white Othello was aimed at questioning the racist production history of the play (Boyle, 2012). Apart from the focus on controversial, mainly German productions, the topic of *Othello*, race and blackface in European countries remains limited. Some attention has been paid to Eastern European productions, where the argument is that they tended to take a more political or romanticised approach to the play, with blackface not being uncommon, in part due to a lack of black actors (Potter, 2002: 200–5). Incidentally, other countries have been highlighted, such as Norway, which employed a white Othello in a production with a military perspective to de-emphasise racial difference aspects and emphasise strain on all military personnel (Thompson, 2016: 83–4).

Generally, the focus on non-anglophone European *Othello*, blackface and casting has been scattered, brief and haphazard, with a focus on Germany, although in that case too only the provocative (at least from an anglophone point of view) productions using white actors were explored. A more detailed analysis of productions in the specific national or cultural context has been lacking, even though it is always argued to be of major importance. Likewise, the relationship between *Othello* productions and cultural blackface traditions in different countries has been an underexplored topic, even though the use of blackface in a variety of countries has continued as part of festivities or cultural expression, despite any controversies. In Germany, for example, the use of blackface is still part of the cultural domain, as seen in the recent Carnival parades, while the tradition is still far stronger in the Netherlands. The interaction between these traditions and their wider cultural and historical context and productions of *Othello* needs further exploration in research that has leaned strongly on an anglophone approach.

This study aims to address some of these issues, moving beyond the anglophone limits, through an in-depth Dutch overview of *Othello* within the national and cultural discourse on race, blackface and theatre. The Netherlands has been chosen for a variety of reasons: like the UK, it participated in the slave trade; it has developed into a multicultural society in the past fifty years; it does not have a lack of black actors; it is closely related to the UK with English being the main foreign language taught in schools and Shakespeare the most performed playwright on stage. It is also a country known traditionally for its tolerant attitude. How then is it possible that white actors and blackface had such a strong presence in the Dutch staging of *Othello* and that there was so little response to the issues of race? Additionally, what can explain this gap between the Netherlands and the USA and the UK, and what effect did the first main house production employing a black actor in 2018 and its rerun in 2020 have on the debate on race and blackface? This Element explores these questions with a focus on the twenty-first century.

The 2018 *Othello* was a brutal and confrontational revelation on the Dutch stage, not only because it employed a black actor, but also because it challenged long-established blackface traditions on and off stage and wanted to address one of the often neglected open wounds on the body of Dutch society, institutional racism. Opposite the black Othello in this production, all the other actors were whitened up even further to highlight the extreme whiteness of the ruling elite. The stage directions which indicated physical abuse by Othello towards Desdemona were spoken by the other characters, but not acted out by Othello. It highlighted how preconceived notions by the white environment of black people's actions, irrespective of whether they had actually taken place, not only influenced but also took over the place of reality. In the end, Othello was strangled by Iago, revealing how exclusion, isolation and marginalisation ultimately led to merciless racial violence. The production, which started out in smaller auditoriums, received raving reviews and had a rerun in 2020 in the big auditoriums throughout the country. Reviewers suddenly noted that 'Othello is black and it matters' (Janssens, 2018), as a representative newspaper headline read. At the same time, the production also got pushback from the Dutch theatre world for choosing racism as the core of the play. Also, while media reaction was positive, the same media continued to deride the very publications on institutional racism which were used as the building blocks for the production. The groundbreaking quality, reception and impact of this production, discussed in detail in Section 5, can be fully understood only in the light of a detailed analysis of the history of migration, multiculturalism and changing attitudes to race and blackface traditions in the Netherlands and of previous productions of *Othello* on the Dutch stage (mainstream and fringe), which follow in Sections 2 to 4.

After a discussion of the political, social and cultural context of blackface and racism in Section 2, the author analyses in Section 3 the tradition of white actors and blackface in *Othello* after World War II, with a focus on Dutch productions in the twenty-first century, including the 2003 Ivo van Hove *Othello*, which had a rerun in 2012. Next, in Section 4, the author analyses the four fringe productions that deviated from this tradition of white actors (with or without blackface) and how both their intent and impact on blackface and the racial discourse were minimal to ambiguous at best. In Section 5, the author analyses the 2018 production and its 2020 rerun, its reception, the implications of this production for future revivals in the Netherlands and, more generally, its impact on the debate about institutional racism and the ongoing controversy about traditions with problematic racist undertones, like Black Pete.

2 Context: Dutch Tolerance, Blackface and Racism

In order to understand the intricate relationship between *Othello*, blackface and race in any national context, be it the UK, the USA or any other country, it is necessary to provide an adequate analysis of the specific historical, political and cultural backgrounds. The Netherlands forms an integral part of the EU, being one of its founding fathers, and is often considered a bastion of tolerance. However, a closer reading of the development of a multicultural Dutch society, blackface traditions and institutional racism may assist in clarifying the more hidden layers. An understanding of this is a *conditio sine qua non* to appreciate the development of the Dutch *Othello* and the discrepancy between the Netherlands and surrounding countries. Before analysing *Othello* productions in more detail, the author first discusses the context, paying specific attention to the Dutch tradition of tolerance, the changing demographic composition, the Dutch role in the slave trade, institutional racism and the blackface tradition of Black Pete.

2.1 A History of Tolerance and Immigration

Four years after Shakespeare was born, William I, Prince of Orange, invaded the Netherlands to drive the Spanish troops out of the country. It was the beginning of the Eighty Years' War, an uprising of seventeen regional states (roughly comprising the present-day Netherlands, Belgium and Luxemburg) against Philip II of Spain. Next to discontent with taxation and an aversion for Spanish absolutism, another major grievance was the religious persecution of Protestants. Dutch society is traditionally known for its tolerance of refugees and outsiders. The Union of Utrecht, a 1579 formal agreement of the northern, more Calvinist provinces in their war against Spain, laid the foundation for the current Netherlands. The agreement guaranteed, for example, that nobody could be persecuted on religious grounds – this amount of religious freedom was unique in Europe at the time (Blom, 1995: 82–92; Griffioen & Zeller, 2011: 165–6; Moore, 1997: 20–3; Poliakov, 1975: 38; Vital, 1999: 61, 145).

In the same year, several of the southern, more Catholic provinces broke away from the northern rebellion against Spain and united in the Union of Atrecht. The war against Spain and the occupation of major cities in these provinces, such as Ghent, Antwerp and Brussels, caused an exodus from the south to the northern city states of Zeeland and Holland. The violence, continuing persecution of Protestants in the Flemish provinces, ongoing pillaging, economic factors and the tolerant political and religious climate in the northern provinces led to many refugees seeking the shelter of the Dutch state. A city such as Antwerp lost, for example, more than half of its inhabitants in this period, while immigrants made up more than half of the population in major Dutch cities such as Leiden, Haarlem and Middelburg. The impact on the young Dutch state was enormous: the economy got a major boost from the new immigrants, many of whom were craftsmen. Art and culture blossomed, and the Netherlands was on the verge of what came to be known as its golden age. After an initially warm welcome, a more negative perception of the immigrants set in. A few decades later, this seemed to have disappeared almost entirely and hardly any references to negative stereotyping against the Flemish could be found anymore (Dubbelman & Tanja, 1987; Lucassen & Penninx, 1999). A new wave of mass immigration caused by religious conflicts was seen at the end of the seventeenth century. In 1685, the Catholic French king Louis XIV revoked the Edict of Nantes, which had offered the Huguenots certain civic and religious freedoms. This led to a renewed persecution of Protestant Huguenots, who sought asylum in surrounding Protestant countries, and more than 50,000 Huguenots migrated to the Netherlands. In this tradition of tolerance, many persecuted Jews also sought shelter in the Dutch state over the centuries, particularly Sephardic Jews from Portugal and Spain and Ashkenazi Jews from Eastern Europe. The strong waves of anti-Semitism that passed over Europe from the second half of the Middle Ages onwards never seemed to have gained a foothold in the Netherlands, and unlike countries such as Russia, Poland, Germany, Great Britain, France and Spain, the Netherlands did not have ghettos, pogroms, job prohibitions or mass expulsions (Blom, 1995: 166–72; Michman, Beem & Michman, 1992: 7–64; Van Andel, 1983: 45–68; Van Arkel, 1984: 47–51).

Apart from refugees, the Netherlands has also known a long tradition of labour migration. From the seventeenth century onwards, tens of thousands of labourers travelled yearly to the Netherlands, usually for seasonal employment in agriculture. Another stream of immigration was made up of trading colonies of foreign merchants, who, contrary to seasonal labourers, generally settled on a more permanent basis in the Netherlands (Heijes, 2001). The first half of the twentieth century saw no large-scale migration to the Netherlands. An important exception was the migration of Belgians to the Netherlands during World War I, but they largely moved back to their home country after the war. Immediately after World War II, during the first few years of reconstruction, the Netherlands experienced a strong surge in emigration to countries such as Canada and Australia. The emigration was strongly stimulated by the Dutch government, which considered the Netherlands overpopulated. At the time, the population was between nine and ten million. By 2019, the Dutch population had increased to more than seventeen million. While this post-war period saw the global perception of Dutch tolerance extended towards lenient attitudes on soft drugs, euthanasia, same-sex marriages and abortion, the fast growth and changing composition of the Dutch population revealed hidden layers underneath the seemingly tolerant Dutch, which partly found their way into *Othello*.

2.2 Recent Migration Patterns

The recent growth of the Dutch population leaned strongly on immigration, which gradually increased after the 1950s. Three new migration groups could be distinguished:

1. Immigrants from former colonies
2. Labour immigrants from the Mediterranean
3. Immigrants who sought political asylum

The former colonies of the Netherlands encompass Indonesia, Surinam and the Netherlands Antilles. Immigration from Indonesia started in 1945, after the capitulation of Japan, and lasted until 1960, partly due to an anti-Dutch mood in Indonesia. The perception at first was that the integration in Dutch society encountered few problems and that most of these immigrants had been warmly welcomed, although later the 'myth of success' was punctured and other stories emerged, emphasising the other side (Ellemers & Vaillant, 1985; Heijes, 2001; Schuhmacher, 1987). Large immigration waves from the former colony of Surinam took place around its independence in 1975 and around 1980, when visas became obligatory. Further deterioration of the Surinam economy, the infamous December murders of 1982 and the increasing sense of military involvement in the country led to the continuation of migration from Surinam to the Netherlands. In total, about a third of the Surinam population left for the Netherlands (Buddingh, 2017). Immigration from the other Dutch colony in the West, the Netherlands Antilles, increased rapidly in the 1970s and 1980s as the economic situation on the Antilles deteriorated. The socio-economically weakest groups on the island suffered most and people fled to the Netherlands, hoping for a better future. Finding a job and a better system of social services were mentioned as causes of migration in the 1970s and 1980s (Heijes, 2003; Koot, 1979).

From the Mediterranean, three main groups migrated to the Netherlands: Southern Europeans, Turks and Moroccans. When the post-war reconstruction gathered steam, the labour market in the Netherlands experienced a shortage of personnel. Companies in sectors such as mining, textile, shipbuilding and also major electronic firms such as Philips recruited employees from countries such as Spain, Italy and Greece to do low-skilled jobs for a couple of years in the Netherlands. As the European labour market became more rigid in the 1960s, recruitment moved to Turkey and Morocco. Although among Southern Europeans there was a high percentage of return migration, most Turkish and Moroccan immigrants remained in the Netherlands (Heijes, 2001; Schuhmacher, 1987; Tinnemans, 1994). From the 1970s onwards, family reunion or marriage with a bride from the mother country increased rapidly, leading to the Mediterranean group in the Netherlands consisting mainly of Turkish and Moroccan immigrants at present. Until the 1970s, unemployment in this group was relatively low but the situation gradually deteriorated. To this day, they remain in a position of disadvantage.

The third group of immigrants was those who sought political asylum. The number of asylum seekers increased drastically from the 1990s onwards. Most of them originated from countries in Africa, Asia and Eastern Europe (*Jaarrapport Integratie*, 2007 *et seq.*; Tesser, Merens & Van Praag 1999). On their arrival, refugees were transferred to asylum centres. The procedure to obtain a refugee 'A status', which closely resembled full citizenship, could take several years. During this period, refugees were not allowed to look for a job and their families could not migrate. More than half of the requests were denied, although only a few refugees were expelled from the Netherlands. Unemployment among this group was high, among not only those without any education, but also those with higher education, as language problems and the fact that diplomas were not always recognised caused many of the refugees to have to start all over again. The perception of asylum seekers has hardened over the past few decades and the increasing flow of immigrants has led to calls for stricter admission policies. The original perception of providing warm hospitality to sincere and brave fighters against dictatorship moved to the background and was gradually replaced by a focus on more negative aspects, such as criminality, emergency accommodation, unemployment and organised human trafficking (Kloosterman, 2018).

L'histoîre se répète? The Netherlands was a country of immigration for much of its history, and over the past fifty years, it has reinstalled itself in this mode. Repeatedly, research has pointed out that the Netherlands used to be a country of immigrants and that history merely repeated itself. In the sixteenth and seventeenth centuries, waves of immigration caused the Dutch population to change; more recently, both economic and political reasons have caused similar migration patterns. Moreover, just as in the past, this increase in immigration has resulted in mixed feelings among the native population. On one hand, people welcomed the immigrants, but on the other, concerns were expressed about the different mentalities and cultures the immigrants brought with them. Just as one stereotyped the Flemish in the sixteenth century or agitated about the 'despicable vices' of the French Huguenots in the seventeenth, the past forty to fifty years have shown a similar concern about immigrants (Dubbelman & Tanja, 1987; *Jaarrapport Integratie*, 2007, *et seq.*).[1]

This, however, is only one part of the story. Although there are significant similarities, there are also differences. Migration in the past was mainly from other European countries, whereas immigrants over the past decades have come from countries outside of Europe. They are no longer the white-faced Flemings and Huguenots who migrated, and immigration from Africa and Asia has caused a visible change in society. Where cultural differences and irritations seemed to disappear in the past, being snowed under in the Dutch climate, there are no clear indications of this happening presently. Moreover, although immigration was relatively high in the past, the current rates are higher than ever before as more than 10 per cent of the Dutch population is of non-Western origin. In the four largest cities in

---

[1] All translations from Dutch to English are by the author. These include personal interviews and citations from written Dutch sources, such as books, journals, published interviews and newspapers.

the Netherlands, almost 40 per cent of youth have parents of non-Western origins. *L'histoîre se répète? L'histoîre se ne répète jamais.* History did not repeat itself as Dutch society was facing new challenges.

Dutch government policy had long focused on the temporary status of immigrants, but the myth of the temporary migrant worker was slowly let go. In the 1990s, integration became the key concept: minorities themselves had to be educated and had to try to integrate into Dutch society (Wet Inburgering, 1998). The new term for these immigrants was the Dutch concept of *allochtoon*, which refers to a person whose parents are not born in the Netherlands, thereby including the second generation. Work, education and integration became the new cornerstones. Whether the policy was successful is up for debate. The formal position of immigrants and their families improved, unemployment decreased, the educational achievement of second-generation immigrants improved, and immigrants were slowly attaining high-level positions.

However, the social and economic position of non-Western immigrants in the Netherlands remained relatively poor. The housing situation was poorer, participation in society was lower, health prospects remained poorer, criminality remained higher and academic research, the Governmental Accounting Office and the Social and Cultural Planning Agency were critical of the effects of government policy (Cozijnsen, Kromhout & Wittkämper, 2019; Day, Klooster & Koçak , 2016; Gielkens & Wegkamp, 2019; Inspectie, 2020; *Jaarrapport Integratie*, 2007 *et seq.*; *Rapportage*, 1993 *et seq.*). The average unemployment rate remains two to three times higher that of the native Dutch. Factors causing this include poor knowledge of the Dutch language, low education levels, limited social integration, which caused migrants to have less access to informal networks in finding a job, and a limited value of foreign education and work experience. However, these factors could not fully explain the high unemployment figures among non-Western migrants, and research has shown continuing discrimination on the labour market to be another important factor (Andriessen, Nievers & Dagevos, 2012; Bovenkerk, 1995; *Jaarrapport Integratie*, 2007 *et seq.*; *Rapport*, 2019; Thijssen, Coenders & Lancee, 2018; Veenman, 1999). Social and economic developments had their impact on perception in the media, and non-Western immigrants became virtually synonymous with problems in the general press: unemployment, school dropouts, criminality, cultural differences and lack of understanding. The media coverage in the Netherlands on ethnic minorities from non-Western countries focused on negative aspects, and there was a gradual move from an appreciatory consideration of multicultural society to a hardening of positions in Dutch politics.

This did not, however, lead to extreme rightist groups in the Netherlands initially, as opposed to countries such as Belgium, France or Austria. In part, this was caused by the minorities' debate in Dutch politics. Political parties gradually moved from an appreciation of multicultural society to an approach wherein assimilation was the keyword and the new minorities had to adapt. In the Netherlands, there would now be space for only one culture – Western culture. Prominent authors from both the left and right spectrums argued that a different cultural background would only result in segregation and poor prospects in Dutch society (Duyvendak & Veldboer, 2001; Prins, 2004). In the aftermath of 9/11 and the assassination in 2002 and 2004 of two criticasters of Dutch multicultural society and Islam, controversial politician Pim Fortuyn and moviemaker Theo van Gogh, who was murdered by Mohammed Bouyeri (a Dutch-Moroccan Muslim), the tone of the debate sharpened and the Dutch showed a growing polarisation. A newly established right-wing party, the PVV, gained a firmer base in the Dutch political landscape, fed by the ongoing migration problems that faced the EU and the Netherlands. The party focused on anti-Islam, anti-European and anti-Moroccan sentiments, caused in part by problems with a small group of Moroccan youngsters. In 2016, a new populist party focusing on immigration issues, the FVD, was established. In 2019, it became the largest political party in the provincial elections while in 2020 it surpassed the Christian Democrat party as the party with the highest level of party members. Although so far, these parties have never gained political responsibility on a national level, their impact on the political debate is unmistakable (*Monitor*, 1997 *et seq.*; Van der Heijden, 2017; Verheul, 2009).

2.3 Racism and Blackface

The terms 'race' and 'ethnicity' are often used interchangeably, with racism becoming incorporated in the concept of ethnicity. Article one of the United Nations International Convention on the Elimination of All Forms of Racial Discrimination (1965) defines racial discrimination as 'any distinction, exclusion, restriction or preference based on race, colour, descent or national or ethnic origin'. In social sciences, 'ethnicity' is generally used to differentiate between people (who originate) from a certain region, incorporating aspects such as nationality, religion, language or specific cultural customs (Barth, 1969; Bentley, 1987; Stone, 1996). 'Race', on the other hand, is traditionally limited to physical characteristics that differentiate groups of people from each other. Over the past decades, critical race scholars have convincingly argued that while race is a social construction with no basis in genetic or scientific research, it has laid the basis for an ongoing process of racialisation and racism, employed to reinforce inequality between people based on arbitrary phenotypic differences, such as skin colour (Allen, 2012; Bonilla-Silva, 2015; Fields & Fields, 2012; Omi & Winant, 2014).

While the wider and more encompassing term 'ethnicity' is frequently used to encompass racism as well, the inverse is also true. Although one of the more recent, extensive studies on discrimination in Dutch society was titled *Dutch Racism* (Essed & Hoving, 2014), its contributors did not apply racism in the traditional sense but rather used the ethnicity approach, including religious, cultural and national discrimination. In her review of the study, Van der Noll (2016: 533) noted how contributors indicated that 'the use of the terms "race" and "racism" is objectionable in the Netherlands, and that, instead, references to "ethnicity" and "ethnic discrimination" are more common'.

Likewise, in the political arena, the racial discourse never seemed to have been an important point of debate. The term 'race' seemed to strike a sensitive nerve in Dutch society and even the more populist parties, such as the PVV or the FVD, rather focused on ethnicity, usually applied in reference to the country of origin or religion. In one of the first studies on racial discrimination in the Netherlands, Essed (1984) argued that structural racism was prominent while the white elite, both left wing and right wing, would be oblivious to any perception of racial problems. Around the turn of the century, the Dutch magazine for multicultural society *Contrast* similarly argued that the Dutch debate on the multicultural society was 'too white' ('Allochtonen', 2000). The seeming inability to specifically address the racial discourse has been attributed partly to the historical Dutch perspective of a tolerant society. The sense of superiority had a long tradition, and in 1944, American anthropologist Ruth

Benedict in a study to prepare American soldiers for their confrontation with the population indicated that no country in Europe was as jealous of its moral rightness as the Netherlands (Benedict, 1944). The tradition of moral righteousness is a recurring theme in studies on Dutch identity (Heijes, 2004; Van Ginkel, 1997), although the conflict with the tradition of Calvinist modesty would not allow this to be expressed too directly, as succinctly described by Oostindie, the director of the Royal Netherlands Institute of Caribbean Studies:

> Deep down, we consider ourselves to be an outstanding people and we particularly consider it to be an outstanding characteristic, that we don't think ourselves to be an outstanding people. And thus, we keep fooling ourselves. (Oostindie, 2002)

More recent studies by Essed and Hoving (2014) and Wekker (2016) supported the argument that the sense of Dutch moral superiority was one of the cornerstones of their racism, which would also result in consistent ignorance, denial or misrepresentation of racial elements in Dutch history. The Dutch were, however, willing and active participants in the global slave trade. Willemstad, harbour of the Dutch colony Curaçao, became an important transit point in the slave trade from West Africa to the New World. The two Dutch monopolist sea trading consortiums, the East and the West Indian Company, which were supported and subsidised by the Dutch government, became major players in colonialism and the slave trade (Heijes, 2004; Vanvugt, 2011).

In the educational system, however, the Dutch colonial role in the slave trade was often glossed over in the curriculum. Even when it was touched upon, it never included references to racism as such (Vanvugt, 2011). Likewise, Hoving (2014: 78–86) argued that despite a series of valuable studies on Dutch migration and colonial history, these often did not specifically discuss racism. Tendayi Achiume (2019), who reported for the UN Human Rights Council on racism in the Netherlands, recently stated in a press conference that she saw an important role for the Dutch government in education to combat racism. Specifically referring to colonial history, she argued that lessons should pay more attention to the Dutch role in the slave trade and colonialism to combat discrimination. A recent movie about Michiel de Ruyter (2015), an admiral in the West Indian Company, illustrated the same. The movie painted the image of a courageous and humane admiral, but critics and demonstrators contended that the movie ignored the admiral's and the Dutch role in the slave trade ('Tientallen', 2015).

In the past couple of years, the racial discourse in Dutch society has intensified as incidents are increasingly reported in the Dutch media and the discussion on racism has entered the general domain. The aforementioned movie about De Ruyter, for instance, also drew a counterdemonstration of members of the Dutch Marine Corps, founded by Michiel de Ruyter around 350 years ago. In 2019, the Amsterdam Museum decided not to use the term 'golden age' anymore for the Dutch seventeenth century, in which the Netherlands was a global superpower, as it ignored many negative aspects such as 'forced labour and slave trade' ('Amsterdams', 2019). This led to heated reactions, and Prime Minister of the Netherlands Mark Rutte (2019) stated that the museum's decision was 'nonsense' and that the Netherlands should be 'incredibly proud' of this period in Dutch history. Later that year, a football match between the First Division teams FC Den Bosch and Excelsior had to be temporarily halted due to racist abuse aimed at Excelsior player Ahmad Mendes Moreira by the home supporters, after which Moreira left the football pitch in tears. Afterwards, Moreira mentioned how he had heard disgusting abuse such as 'cancer-*neger*, cancer cotton picker, cancer black and Black Pete'. The trainer of FC, Den Bosch, initially called Moreira a 'sad little man' while the home team argued that they were just ordinary 'crow sounds'. The news of this incident spread across the world, after which the Dutch Football Association launched an investigation and both the Excelsior trainer and the home team quickly withdrew their statements after the match, offering sympathy and deciding to launch an investigation of their own into the racism ('Den Bosch', 2019). Half a year later, the Dutch cabinet decided to free a budget to combat racism in football and the Football Association argued that its board was too 'white; we need to become more diverse' (Winterman, 2020).

One of the most recent incidents, at the time of writing, related to a Dutch pastry. In 2020, a Dutch bakery changed the name of one of its pastries, a circular chocolate éclair, from the traditional Dutch name 'Moor's Head' to

'Cream's Head', after some customers complained. The change resulted in an outpouring of criticism on social media and the owner closed the shop because of a client's aggression, insisting that he wanted a 'Moor's Head'. Members of the Dutch Bread and Bakery Association argued it was the first time they had heard of such a subject, but the national Dutch warehouse HEMA followed suit and changed the name of the delicacy to 'Chocolate Roll'. The owner of the bakery was accused on social media of destroying Dutch traditions and being a 'traitor to his country, a member of the NSB [a fascist political party that collaborated with the Germans during the Second World War] and a leftist fool' (Verwoerd, 2020). At the same time, the largest newspaper of the Netherlands, the right-wing *Telegraaf*, spoke of opportunistic and overanxious multicultural behaviours of shop owners (Kalkman, 2020). Such defensive, argumentative or minimising reactions, once the topic of racism is brought up, are also referred to as 'white fragility' (DiAngelo, 2018). In reference to the Dutch context, Nzume (2017a) indicated how white fragility determined the strong and emotional reactions of many Dutch people to accusations of racism, irrespective of class or political preference.

2.4 Black Pete

The most prominent and controversial example of the sensitivity of the topic in the Netherlands, which also relates to blackface, is the debate surrounding the Dutch tradition of Black Pete. In the traditional festivity, the birthday of Saint Nicholas is celebrated every year on 5 December by giving gifts to children. Two to three weeks before his birthday, Saint Nicholas, dressed in red robes and with a long white beard, arrives from Spain by boat, accompanied by hundreds of 'Black Petes'. They are generally white persons with blackened faces, wearing large golden rings in their ears, with curly black wigs and accented red lips, dressed in bright and colourful clothes. In the period leading up to 5 December, Saint Nicholas travels over the roofs on his white horse, accompanied by these servants, who drop off gifts for children through chimneys. During these weeks, Saint Nicholas and his Black Petes also visit virtually all primary schools as well as many working places, where more gifts are distributed. Children sing a variety of songs which include lines such as 'even though I am black as soot, I still mean it well' or references to the fact that if you did not behave well, Black Pete would hit you, put you in a bag and carry you away. This festivity is far more important than Father Christmas and is the major Dutch family festivity of the year.

The Dutch tradition of the Catholic Saint Nicholas dates back to the Middle Ages, while the character of Black Pete has often been associated with Indo-European traditions of devilish characters with a mixture of black masks, horns, black faces and black clothes who would occasionally accompany a white, grey-haired man bearing gifts. In the Netherlands, from the beginning of the nineteenth century onwards, Saint Nicholas was occasionally portrayed as accompanied by a servant, generally black. The tradition was given a further boost by the publication of an illustrated children's book by Schenkman (1850), which introduced the arrival of Saint Nicholas in the Netherlands by steamboat from Spain and which contained many illustrations of a colourfully dressed black servant assisting him (Booy, 2014; Brienen, 2014; Helsloot, 2008). In the same period, American blackface minstrelsy was introduced to the Dutch public and became a standard element of the theatre repertoire. While arguably the tradition of Black Pete may not have been directly related to minstrelsy, its influence was unmistakable and in the second half of the nineteenth century the Dutch character of Black Pete increasingly adopted elements of minstrelsy (Brienen, 2014; Koning, 2018). Criticism on the inherent racism in the tradition has slowly increased and escalated, over the past decade, into confrontations between advocates and opponents of the tradition.

In 2013, Verene Shepherd, a professor at the University of the West Indies, spoke out against the tradition of Black Pete. She was part of a committee of five persons who investigated racism in the Netherlands for the United Nations' Working Group of Experts on People of African Descent. The group also evaluated the tradition of Black Pete, which it deemed outdated, and the Black Pete character, which it considered a racist stereotype of black people connected with Dutch colonial history. They said it implied a relationship of servitude and inferiority of black persons to white. Four years later, she revealed that, ever since, she had been continuously receiving hate mail from Dutch persons who opposed any change in the tradition of Black Pete.

She added that there came a point when the amount of hate mail coming in was so huge that the university's servers crashed (Shepherd, 2017).

In 2016, the national Dutch ombudsperson for children reported that the character of Black Pete conflicted with the international Convention on the Rights of the Child. The character would contribute to bullying, exclusion and discrimination, and she reported that many coloured children experienced a worsening of discrimination during these festivities (Kalverboer, 2016a). Like Shepherd, she received many threats, including death threats which caused her to file a report with the police (Kalverboer, 2016b). While some towns have made changes and reduced the amount of blackface, or even introduced Blue or Yellow Petes, the changes are scattered and the national petitions to maintain the tradition of Black Pete have drawn millions of votes. In 2017, Frisian Black Pete supporters blocked a highway with their cars to prevent several buses with anti-Black Pete supporters from demonstrating the arrival of Saint Nicholas (Bahara & Ezzeroili, 2019). In 2018, the *Telegraaf*, which has the highest circulation of all the newspapers in the Netherlands, fully supported the tradition on pages one, two and three of its edition:

> Rutte [the prime minister] calls upon everyone to go to the arrivals [of Saint Nicholas] in the entire country. Because the festivities will continue, in the hope that the joyful singing of children will override the pestering. ('Hij komt', 2018)

A year later, Tendayi Achiume (2019), Shepherd's successor for the UN in the Netherlands, stated that the Dutch government should take the lead both in fighting racism and in the Black Pete debate, referring to the role of Prime Minister Rutte, who argued that this was not a national responsibility. The recent death of George Floyd and the Black Lives Matter movement, which also resulted in demonstrations across the Netherlands, impacted this debate directly, while simultaneously revealing the ongoing ambivalence in the discourse on racism. In a parliamentary debate, Prime Minister Rutte (2020) indicated that his thinking on Black Pete had changed due to current events, that he was now more aware of the pain some people might feel at the tradition, that he wanted to engage in a further discussion with opponents, and that he thought the tradition might naturally evolve and change in the coming years. On the other hand, he also argued that the tradition was not inherently racist and maintained that it is not the responsibility of the central government to initiate change.

The debate on the tradition of Black Pete remains a troublesome and contentious spot in Dutch society that has brought Dutch racism to the surface and that keeps attracting international attention, as indicated earlier in the first paragraph of this Element. The most recent voice in the increasing chorus criticising the Dutch tradition is that of US civil rights leader Jesse Jackson, who wrote a personal letter to the Dutch prime minister on Black Pete:

> As the whole world mourns the brutal murder of George Floyd, followed by the worldwide mass protest demonstrations calling for actions to combat racism, I do not think it was appropriate for you to explain that you understand better the sufferings of black people regarding Black Pete and at the same time, saying that you do not consider Black Pete as racist. (Jackson, 2020)

Jackson urged Rutte to abolish the tradition of Black Pete for good, calling it 'a racist relic of colonialism' that 'cannot be separated from the very offensive tradition of black face', while quoting Martin Luther King in saying that there 'are times when it's appropriate to be political, but sometimes it's more important to be prophetic – to just do what's right' (Jackson, 2020). It is against the background of the historical and cultural context described in this section that Dutch productions of *Othello* have to manoeuvre and respond. How they did or failed to do so, and how the 2018 production and its 2020 rerun might have marked a watershed, are discussed next.

3 Othello after World War II: White Actors and Blackface

In the next three sections, the author analyses how Dutch productions of *Othello* have responded to the changing demographic composition and to what extent they have engaged with blackface and the racial discourse. In this section, the focus is on the continued use of white actors, with or without blackface, in the title role on the Dutch stage. After a brief introduction to the post-war *Othello* tradition on the Dutch stage, the author analyses the Ivo van Hove 2003 production and its rerun in 2012 as well as the 2015 *Othello* by Servé Hermans in more detail, both of which used white actors, a provocative translation with racial slurs and different variations on blackface.

3.1 Post-war Othello: Blackface and White Actors

Although the main focus of this study is the twenty-first-century approach to *Othello*, a brief overview of eight important *Othello* productions in the Netherlands in the second half of the twentieth century is provided, as they formed the frame of reference which twenty-first-century productions built on and responded to. These productions include the 1951 *Othello* by Rotterdams Toneel, directed by Frits van Dijk; the 1964 Haagsche Comedie, directed by Bob de Lange; the 1971 and 1988 Globe productions directed by Leo van Hensbergen and Ronald Klamer respectively; the 1989 Shakespeare Theatre Diever, directed by Wil ter Horst-Rep; the 1993 Toneelgroep Amsterdam, directed by Johan Simons; the 1996 Noord Nederlands Toneel (hereafter NNT) by Karst Woudsta; and the 1997 Stella production, directed by Alize Zandwijk. The most remarkable finding from the perspective of blackface is that the approach hardly changed during this long time frame. Where developments in the USA, the UK and Germany had led to the demise or critical interrogation of blackface, the introduction of actors of colour for the title role and increased attention to the racial discourse, these developments were virtually absent in Dutch *Othello* productions. Throughout the period, white actors were used, and the use of blackface was not critically interrogated by directors, actors or reviewers.

The persistent use of blackface in this period did not elicit any critical response unless it referred to the craftsmanship of the make-up or the lack of it. Blackface was considered a fascinating and useful, but also an obvious technique that was applied unquestioningly in productions of *Othello*. Initially, comments such as 'magnificent make-up, not too black, a Moor is a Berber, not a *neger*' ('*Othello* bij het Rotterdams', 1951) or 'wonderfully applied brown make-up' (Hartering, 1964) might not have differed from anglophone productions. From the 1970s onwards, however, the divergence became more noticeable. Productions in the 1980s elicited no response at all to the use of blackface (de Vries, 1989; Straatman, 1988), while in the last two productions of the 1990s, it was as if time had come to a complete standstill. Reviews of *Othello*, in outlets across the political spectrum, were worded in a manner that would be considered not only outdated and politically incorrect, but also downright offensive in anglophone countries. The 1996 production, in which blackface covered the entire body – visible in the final scene, when Othello, after killing Desdemona, committed necrophilia on Desdemona's corpse – led to a reviewer commenting how the audience could have a good look at 'the carelessly blackened up but beautiful butt crack of Othello' (Zonneveld, 1996).

A year later, in Stella's production, the blackface was described as 'a firm amount of pitch-black shoe polish on his body, which spread over to anyone he touched' (Schaap, 1997). A similar use of blackface in Zadek's 1976 *Othello* in Germany was instead used to interrogate racist topics. However, while Zadek's production was popular in Germany, and is often mentioned in handbooks and performance overviews, Zadek had only one show in the Netherlands at the time, with a mixed reception. Even the more positive reviews fully ignored the contemporary racial dimensions (de Groot, 1977; de Lange, 1977; Van den Bergh, 1977). Not much had changed in the Netherlands twenty years later. The only production to not use blackface in this time frame was the 1993 *Othello*, in which the actor was whitened up even further and was made to wear a black costume for differentiating. The actor had experimented with brownface and blackface during the rehearsals, but decided to use a dark costume in the end (Van Uffelen, 1993). For the director, it was irrelevant, as both his and the actor's focus was on the outsider in general and racial topics had no specific place in the play (Simons, 1993). Likewise, reviewers firmly focused on the role of the outsider, and although the production changed its approach to casting Othello without blackface, this hardly resulted in any critical reflection on blackface or racial (or even ethnic) topics in *Othello* (Hellmann, 1993; Schouten, 1993).

Ironically, the 1951 production, before the emergence of Dutch multicultural society, arguably introduced the relevance of racial and ethnic contrasts more than any other twentieth-century production afterwards. To the director, the differences in culture, religion and skin colour marked Othello an outsider and easy prey to Iago's insinuations. In the difference between 'the converted Catholic dignitary of a white society' and the 'Muslim barbarian, . . . offended in his honour', the director saw an almost inevitable path to Desdemona's murder (Van Dijk, 1951). In a similar vein, the director of the 1971 production argued that cultural differences between the 'Western, rational world' and the 'magical world' of Othello were a determining factor in his downfall (Van Hensbergen, 1970). The topics of race, culture, ethnicity and religion were used rather stereotypically and interchangeably by these directors and were hardly picked up in the reviews of the production, which focused on the star-acting and the 'universal' love tragedy (Carmiggelt, 1951; Heyn, 1951; Hofstra, 1951; Boswinkel, 1971; de Lange, 1971; Spierdijk, 1971).

As the Dutch multicultural society evolved, one might have expected a firmer focus on racial or ethnic issues and the growing tensions in the Netherlands due to changing migration patterns and demographic composition. However, any specific references to the Dutch context or attempts to address these present-day tensions were rather limited and superficial in these productions. Even though in 1988, the newly coined Dutch term *allochtoon* was first used in *Othello*, any attempt to relate the play to Dutch multicultural society was absent (Zeeman, 1988). Othello was rather seen as a love tragedy, addressing the topics of jealousy and passion on a personal level (Buijs, 1988; de Ruiter, 1988; Van de Harst, 1988). Further, a year later, the next director of *Othello* defined it as a 'domestic tragedy, in which everyone recognizes so much because they can truly sympathize with the victim' (ter Horst-Rep, 1989). The 1993 production, without any blackface, did not reflect on any ethnic or racial issues in Dutch society, but rather presented Othello and Desdemona both as outsiders in a tragedy of jealousy, with only one reviewer briefly arguing that 'cultural differences' might be the essence of the play (Schouten, 1993). These types of passing comments were also part of the 1996 production, where Othello was seen as a Dutch Antillean, but, once again, *Antillean* appeared mainly as a descriptive term and not as a springboard for deeper explorations of racism or tensions with Antilleans in Dutch society (Zonneveld, 1996). Although gradually some references to multicultural society emerged, they were fleeting, superficial or stereotypical and were generally seen as a distraction from the core of the play. While Othello's outsider status was always an element in these productions, this status was generally not connected to any specific contemporary comments, and Othello was rather seen as a vehicle for generalised human emotions. He functioned as a kind of Everyman. In line with this, reviewers also focused on this core (Freriks, 1997; Hellman, 1993; Schaap, 1997; Schouten, 1993), while the 1996 *Othello*, which included an element of slapstick humour, was criticised for straying too far from the love tragedy (Buijs, 1996; Geerlings, 1996).

3.2 Ivo van Hove, Bouazza and the Outsider

The trend towards focusing on the outsider, which was already visible in many of the productions of previous decades, continued and further increased in the twenty-first century. While these productions still saw *Othello* mainly as a play about jealousy and general human emotions, the focus was stronger than before on Dutch multicultural society and the problems it faced. At the same time, racial issues, a debate on casting a white actor as Othello or the use of blackface remained on the fringes of these productions and their reception, even though the modern translations were blatantly brutal and composed of far stronger racist stereotyping than ever before. The gulf with other countries became ever more significant in main house productions of the twenty-first century, although these productions did build on stage history in the Netherlands and corresponded to a general tendency in Dutch society, on both sides of the political spectrum, to turn a blind eye to the topic of racism. Next, the 2003 *Othello*, directed by Ivo van Hove, and the 2015 *Othello*, directed by Servé Hermans, are discussed in detail, while also briefly touching upon the rerun of the 2003 *Othello* in 2012 and the 2006 *Othello* by Johan Doesburg.

From the 1960s onwards, theatre companies increasingly used translations specifically written for the stage by well-known Dutch authors. A prominent example is Dutch poet Bert Voeten, who translated seven Shakespeare plays (1951–64), mainly for the Dutch theatre company Haagsche Comedie, although many other companies also used his translations. Another well-known Dutch writer who translated Shakespeare was Gerrit Komrij, who was originally supposed to translate all of Shakespeare's plays but stopped after fifteen translations (1981–95). His translations were still used in the twenty-first century, although many directors switched to translations written for one specific production. This resulted in many Dutch Shakespeare translations being currently relatively close to the modern language and forming an almost integral part of the production and the director's vision of the play. Van Hove indicated the advantage of this, which 'the English and Americans will be jealous of. Our first choice as a director these days is: what kind of translation do you want? It is a choice which they do not have' (Van Hove, 2012: 46). For his *Othello*, Van Hove asked Dutch Moroccan Hafid Bouazza to write the script (Bouazza, 2003). Bouazza, born 1970, is a Moroccan Dutch author and translator whose father moved to the Netherlands as a migrant worker in 1971, followed by his family six years later. Bouazza had worked earlier with Van Hove on a translation for the stage of Christopher Marlowe's *The Massacre at Paris* (Bouazza, 2001).

For Bouazza, Othello was an Arab, a Moroccan, which corresponded both with his background and with that of Dutch society, wherein Moroccans formed one of the largest groups of ethnic minorities. As discussed before, a small group of criminal Moroccan youngsters received a large amount of attention in the media debate on the challenges of Dutch multicultural society. In order to present Othello as an Arab Moroccan outsider, Bouazza enhanced racial and ethnic differences between the white Venetians and Othello in several ways, presenting him as more dignified while highlighting the possible cultural background of his actions and emphasising the racial discrimination he encountered in Venice.

On one hand, the text used relatively neutral terms to indicate Othello's provenance by translating 'Moor' as 'Saracen', 'Arab' or 'Maghrebian'. On the other hand, the translation went much further than the original text in highlighting the racial discrimination towards Othello by using a wide variety of expressions for him, some of them very abusive and racist, which highlighted not only Othello's Arab ethnicity, but also his darker skin colour. Thus, Othello was referred to in the translation as a 'camel', 'sand *neger*', 'stupid *nikker*', 'shining smokestack' and 'desert rat'.[2] Although the term was geographically incorrect, 'scorched Tartar' also described him (Bouazza, 2003). In the Dutch language, this can be used as an abusive term, but it also indicates a darkly burnt piece of beef and additionally refers to an originally Turkish person living in Russia. In a reference to the Dutch multicultural society and the Amsterdam context of the theatre company, Othello was also called a 'Naffer', a Dutch contraction of 'North African', a term police officers in Amsterdam first used in the 1990s while dealing with Moroccan delinquents. The extremely abusive terms used in the translation clearly set Othello apart from the other characters and focused on a difference in ethnicity as well as race. When Emilia found out that Othello had killed Desdemona, she used a term that is considered highly offensive and racist among the Dutch. The sentence 'Thou dost belie her, and thou art a devil' (5.2.131)[3] was translated as 'You vilify her and you are a *nikker*'

---

[2] The Dutch word *neger* is typically translated in English as *negro*, and *nikker* is the Dutch version of the n-word. Over the past decades the Dutch word *neger*, originating from the seventeenth century in connection with the slave trade and referring to black people from sub-Saharan Africa, has increasingly been considered an offensive term, although some still argue that the word is merely a neutral term, as is suggested in its frequent use in the journalistic reviews cited here. The Dutch word *nikker* is considered highly offensive and is seen as one of the most insulting and racist terms one can use in Dutch. In this particular instance, and in many other instances in this Element, the Dutch translators of *Othello* have used both terms, *neger* and *nikker*, purposefully and at times almost indiscriminately, in order to highlight the racial abuse Othello had to undergo. While these terms are understood as extremely offensive in Dutch, it might be said – as the entire Black Pete controversy witnesses – that there is a different sensitivity to the iteration of these terms as itself an act of injury, reproducing both racism and its consequences, than there is in the United States. As a way to respond to these cultural and historical politics, I have chosen to leave the Dutch terms untranslated here.

[3] References to *Othello* are based on *The Arden Shakespeare Othello*, ed. by E. A. J. Honigmann with a new introduction by Ayanna Thompson (London: Bloomsbury, 2016).

(Bouazza, 2003: 205). Although the term refers in Dutch to black people from sub-Saharan Africa, which does not include Morocco, the earlier reference in the text to 'sand *neger*' indicated that it could apply to this Arab Othello as well. It is one of the most insulting terms that one can use in Dutch and was part of a continuous process of abuse which highlighted Othello's status as a highly discriminated against Arab outsider.

Another major change in the translation was the addition of lines by Bouazza aimed at enhancing Othello's nobility by weaving Arabic stories into his monologues. When Othello described his background, the translator added, derived from Arab poetry, lyrical passages with beautiful metaphors of medieval Arab poets, such as Abu Tayyib al-Mutanabbi, Antarah Ibn Shaddad and Ta'abata Sharran. Their fantasy and imagery wove an almost *One Thousand and One Nights*–like enchantment, which provided this Othello with a distinct cultural background and past. From these Arab-based texts, readers and viewers of the play also learned that Othello used to be a slave in Franconia who had gained freedom by serving his master very well in numerous battles against adversaries who were his former countrymen: 'And I attacked – as thousands [of] battles may testify/I fought enemies who once/Shared heart and soul with me and faith' (Bouazza, 2003: 36). The audience also learned that he was ridiculed for his skin colour by the girls in his village when he was young, which might indicate, as a reviewer suggested, that he was an Arab *neger* slave, further adding to his isolation (Takken, 2003a).

Othello's different Arab background was, according to the translator, a major cause for his behaviour. In a translation that included no fewer than 157 notes and four appendices, Bouazza argued how Othello's assimilation was only superficial and hid his Arab descent, which Bouazza saw as aggressive and superstitious. An example was when Othello compared Desdemona's handkerchief to her honour: 'She is protectress of her honour too:/May she give that?' (4.1: 14–15). In a footnote to the translation, Bouazza added, 'A remark like this one is very typical for an Arab. This kind of rhetoric hides a rambling logic: a handkerchief is, for many reasons, not the same as "honour"' (Bouazza, 2003: 138). In an earlier scene, Othello described the special provenance of the handkerchief and its magical properties:

'Tis true, there's magic in the web of it.
A sibyl that had numbered in the world
The sun to course two hundred compasses,
In her prophetic fury sewed the work;
The worms were hallowed that did breed the silk,
And it was dyed in mummy, which the skilful
Conserved of maiden's heart. (3.4: 71–7)

Although the translation followed Shakespeare's lines quite closely, a footnote to these lines was far from sympathetic: 'Othello applied similar seduction techniques as other foreigners in the heyday of twentieth-century exotic immigrants: talking crap about the magic of the country of origin. The days one could win a woman's northern heart and her unmade bed with those kinds of stories are gone' (Bouazza, 2003: 128). While on one hand the translation lent dignity to Othello by adding beautiful, poetic lines to his monologues, on the other hand the translator took a generalising and reductive approach to Othello's Arab background in direct references to recent migration patterns. Likewise, in the same scene, similar footnotes were added as Othello said, 'This hand of yours requires/A sequester from liberty, fasting and prayer,/Much castigation exercise devout' (3.4: 39–41). In two footnotes, the translator added 'Othello's Arab nature surfaces' and 'Muslims will nod in agreement' (Bouazza, 2003: 126).

In line with the translation, in this production, Othello was visually presented as an Arab, which was realised by the application of make-up on a white actor. Hans Kesting, who played Othello, had brown make-up all over his body, and in an interview before the opening night, Kesting and the interviewer commented on this choice:

> Tonight [Kesting] plays the title role in *Othello*, this time not in blackface, but as a Moroccan in an American uniform . . . Usually the tragic hero is black, but this colour was not appropriate according to Kesting: 'Othello is a North African, maybe someone from Morocco, and North Africans tend to be brown with a hint of yellow. It turned

> out to be quite difficult to apply this type of make-up to my
> body. (Kesting, 2003)

The tradition of a white actor with blackface or brownface was, as we saw
earlier, the traditional approach to *Othello* in the twentieth century, and
Kesting's comments revealed the unquestioning approach to the custom.
While in the UK and the USA, having white actors – let alone white actors
in blackface – play Othello was by now a rarity, in the Netherlands, it was still
common practice, and the Van Hove production was no exception to this. Any
awareness of a debate or critical reflection on the use of blackface was absent
and the focus for Kesting was on the technical aspect of make-up and on
Othello's Arab background. Othello's Arab roots, well discussed in critical
literature as one of the options for identifying Othello, found their way both in
the translation and in the brown make-up of the main actor.

The strong concentration on race and culture in the translation did not
result in a questioning of the practice of blackface as such, and critical
comments on skin colour were also absent in its reception, which, like
Kesting's remarks, zoomed in in a neutral manner on the use of brown
make-up, the Arab character Kesting was meant to represent and the
tradition of blackface: 'In many productions of *Othello*, the protagonist
had make-up applied which was pitch-black, but Hans Kesting's Othello is
light brownish. More of a Mediterranean type' (Prinssen, 2003). Virtually
all reviewers reported in a similarly neutral tone on the practice, except for a
few dissenting voices. A reviewer from a Christian newspaper argued
against the use of make-up and reflected on the Dutch *Othello* of 1993, in
which Rick van Uffelen played the role without blackface, but was whitened
up even further, as mentioned before. Both approaches were deemed super-
fluous by the reviewer, for whom this was only a minor point of attention in
an otherwise 'fantastic' performance by Kesting:

> Just one small bit of criticism. Hans Kesting had brown
> make-up applied from top to toe. Is that really necessary?
> . . . Seeing that it is already mentioned in the beginning that
> Othello is 'the Moor', surely there is no need to smear
> yourself like that? (Oranje, 2003)

While the comments seemed to argue that make-up of any kind would not be necessary at all for a white actor, the writer added, 'Let us hope that among our countrymen of the Mediterranean type, there will soon be those who are as good in acting as Bouazza is in writing' (Oranje, 2003). Although the comment was made rather condescendingly and within the context of using white actors without make-up, it was the first time the issue was mentioned. On a more serious note, the new director of Cosmic Theatre, Khaldoun Elmecky, criticised the Dutch theatre as too white, unable and unwilling in general to establish a culturally more diverse theatre: 'Theatre is first and foremost recognition. People who are not from the Netherlands, in Amsterdam almost half the population, do not recognise themselves in the current white theatre' (Elmecky, 2003). Focusing on Van Hove's *Othello* in particular, he argued that 'an *Othello* with Theatre Company Amsterdam will always be a white *Othello*, even if they hire an Arab director or some black actors' (Elmecky, 2003). However, these few attempts at initiating a debate on casting decisions or on racial issues in *Othello* (and the Dutch stage in general) were virtually drowned out by the overwhelming and almost uncritical enthusiasm the production engendered.

While the production did not deviate from previous Dutch productions in its casting of Othello, it did deviate in the translation it used and the way it highlighted Othello's different ethnic and racial backgrounds and the references to Dutch multicultural society. One would expect reception of the production to pay attention to this as well, and to some extent it did. Most reviewers described Othello as a successful Arab migrant or compared him to Colin Powell, and a few argued that 'racial hatred' (Bobkova, 2003) or 'hatred of foreigners' (Smith, 2003) was an undertone. Most reviewers, however, limited this undertone to a description of the translation, rather than integrating it into their analysis of the production as a whole. Bouazza's translation was generally applauded, especially the added Arab verses and the many translations of the word 'Moor' which helped set Othello apart from his surroundings:

> With Bouazza, Othello is more than ever a discriminated Arab. He is a stranger who is never sure of his position. Together with his jealousy, the furious 'desert man' would

emerge from underneath the thin veneer of civilisation, obsessed with honour and revenge. From a man, he turns into a racist stereotype. (Takken, 2003b)

The difference between Othello's culture and Western culture was a recurring theme, although in reviews too it was discussed in reductive and stereotypical terms. This cultural background was mainly connected to manhood and honour, and one of the reviews drew a parallel with 'the current commotion about how North African men treated their wives' (Zonneveld, 2003: 57). In the review, Bouazza himself confirmed this approach: 'I turned Othello into a proper Arab, a man who understands nothing about women' (Zonneveld, 2003: 57). Even Othello's corruption by Iago was explained in this context as Van Hove and Bouazza pointed out Othello's language deficiency, particularly important as in Arab culture the word was important and not the imaginative power of the word, which would make Othello extra susceptible to Iago's insinuations (Bouazza, 2003: 120; Van Hove, 2003).

However, although the translation caused a shift in the increased attention on Othello's outsider status, the reception of the production as a whole remained rather fixed on other aspects. Many reviews focused on the masculine and military world in which Othello moved, determining his dysfunctional relationship with Desdemona (Bobkova, 2003; de Jong, 2003a; Janssen, 2003; Nederpelt, 2003; Oranje, 2003; Takken, 2003b). The first scene of the production – situated in a gym, with four half-naked men recuperating from boxing and dressing afterwards in military costume – set the tone for this hardened and rigid world. Other dominant themes in reception included domestic tragedy, situated in a glass house on stage, never free from outside eyes, jealousy, the outsider and the Fall of Man. Roeland Fernhout, who played Iago, argued that the production was essentially 'about friendship and relationships and all the things that happen between persons' (Fernhout, 2003). Van Hove added the subtitle 'Can love save the world?' to the production, and for Kesting, playing Othello, this signified the core of the play. Even the translator of the play argued that 'not racism, not revenge, not jealousy, but misdirection [was] the main theme of the play' (Bouazza, 2003: 10). Most criticisms on the acclaimed production focused on the light female roles (de Jong, 2003b; ten Bruggencate, 2003) rather than on any discourse of racism, Arab discrimination or the use of a white actor with brown make-up. While the translation as such was applauded, it was done so in an ambiguous manner and did not result in any debate on stereotyping or race. Even the lone reviewer who criticised the production as too discriminatory did not do so to engage in a debate or to point out the essentialist approach, but only because it distracted from the core of the production:

> Obviously, the Dutch Moroccan Bouazza does not hold his former countrymen in high esteem. But his vision is rather limited. *Othello* is a universal masterpiece about envy and misdirection. Trying to turn this into a multicultural drama with a message of 'once an Arab, always an Arab' discredits the play entirely. (Takken, 2003a)

Two productions used the same translation: a rerun of Van Hove's production in 2012 and one directed by Johan Doesburg in 2006. While the 2006 production by theatre company Het Nationale Toneel used the same Bouazza translation, it changed the make-up for the actor. In this production, Othello appeared on stage with blackface and in the beginning, he removed the blackface with a white handkerchief to, the actor argued, symbolise Othello's integration into the white world (Römer, 2006). While the 2003 production had used brownface purposefully to indicate Othello's Arab background, the use of blackface this time indicated only the seeming irrelevance of blackface versus brownface in determining Othello's outsider status or Arab background. Both actor and director stated that 'Othello's skin colour is only a minor issue' (Doesburg, 2020; Römer, 2006). The main thing was that Othello was different. On the use of blackface as such, there was no critical reflection at all, and the reviews of the production also centred on the loss and vulnerability of beauty and love in a world of outsiders longing for affection (Freriks, 2006; Veraart, 2006).

In a rerun of the Van Hove production in 2012, with the original cast, same translation and Arab approach, a notable change was that the make-up was fully removed, which led to the visual discrepancy of white actor Kesting being confronted with ethnic and racial discrimination. For Van

Hove, the decision not to use brownface was also influenced by the desire to avoid a focus on only one affiliation, in this case, race, to the detriment of other affiliations, such as ethnicity and class (Massai, 2018: 24). Looking back at the 2003 *Othello*, Van Hove (2012: 47) stated that it was also his intent to bring across how populist parties, such as the Dutch PVV, handily used base emotions to stereotype and discriminate against outsiders, just as Iago did. However, this was not readily recognised in the 2003 reviews, as Van Hove admitted: 'Perhaps we were too early. Still, *Othello* was the first production which was really popular in Amsterdam' (Van Hove, 2012: 47). While one may wonder about the inability to recognise this in 2003, when populist parties and xenophobia had already become mainstream in the political and media landscape, the expectation that things would be different now did not materialise either. Neither the 2006 introduction of blackface nor the removal of brownface as well as Van Hove's renewed intent on topical relevance seemed to impact the play's reception, which was now focused on Othello as a tragedy of love, jealousy and slander, perhaps even more so than in 2003 (Akveld, 2015; Zonneveld, 2012).

3.3 The 2015 Open-Air Othello: Another Outsider

The final production explored in this section, coming after the 2012 rerun of the Van Hove *Othello*, is the 2015 open-air production of *Othello* by theatre company Maastricht, one of the major regional theatre companies in the Netherlands. The company commissioned Jibbe Willems, a well-known theatre translator in the Netherlands, to translate the play (Willems, 2015). Like Bouazza, Willems aimed at increasing and strengthening the instances of racist verbal abuse Othello would have to undergo. Where the Van Hove production chose Arab roots, this production opted for an African background that found its way into the translation as well. The translator used phrases such as 'the horny Moor', 'the filthy pitch black paws', 'those *negers* are never monogamous', 'African cockroach', 'barbarian immigrant', 'that coalface', 'a talking gorilla', 'this primitive creature' and 'bushman' (Willems, 2015). It was another brutal translation of the play demonstrating the ugly face of racism, following in Bouazza's footsteps. What was new was a specific reference to Black Pete, thereby connecting it directly to the tradition of Saint

Nicholas in Dutch society. In his translation of Iago's line 'And I, God bless the mark, his Moorship's ancient!' (1.1.32), the translator made Iago refer to himself as 'the servant of Black Pete' (Willems, 2015: 8). In this, the production went beyond the 2003 *Othello*, which was far less focused on racial issues. Willems, however, explicitly indicated that one of the topics he wanted to address in his translation was racism in Dutch society:

> I want to address the debate on racism firmly. What the discussions on Black Pete, institutional racism in the police, the judicial system, the labour market and the haggling about the word '*neger*' have revealed (irrespective of one's position in the debate) is the presence of a slumbering but very aggressive racism underneath the Dutch epidermis . . . Since some people protested the racist aspects of a children's tradition, xenophobic hatred has popped up like pus from a wound. Not implicitly, not behind one's back and in its small, hidden ugliness, but blunt, large, and smeared all over the social media. (Willems, 2015: 146–7)

The production used a white actor for the role of Othello, but the first scene of the play showed him walking on stage in a black mask, eating a banana and afterwards playing the jazzy bass. It immediately set the tone with a series of stereotypes about black people, which was further reinforced by the translation. However, after the first glimpses of Othello on stage, the black mask was removed and he returned on stage in a bow tie, white shirt and black suit, similar to other white actors, seemingly assimilated and with no visible hint of his race. The obvious idea behind this was that visible characteristics would have determined one's perception and judgement of the other, and the now white Othello would always remain an outsider in this world. It made for an odd contrast with the racial harshness of the translation, and director Servé Hermans (2015a) indicated that it was mainly his intent to present Othello as an outsider, rather than focusing on the racial aspect as such. The company had its roots in Limburg, a province that used to be the wealthiest on account of the coal industry but is now one of the poorest in the Netherlands. It is the southernmost province, and the populist PVV has an extraordinarily strong hold there. In 2017, the PVV became the largest political party in the province. Hermans stressed the inferiority complex in the province due to the economic downturn and wanted to address how a closed community such as this one would cope with outsiders. He called it 'soft racism':

> When someone from outside passes through, it has to be stressed that he is different. The same thing happens to the black Othello. He is a successful general and is condoned for what he can do, but in the meantime, the entire Venetian community is fully aware that 'he is not one of us.' That too is an aspect of Limburg. That is something I really wanted to show. (Hermans, 2015a)

In this approach, race by itself was less of an issue; however, being an outsider was an issue which also became clear as Hermans indicated his own experience in this area. He was born in Limburg and had worked in Ghent (Belgium) for a while. He mentioned how every day everyone, even his best friends, called him 'the Hollander', considering him an outsider for a Belgian position:

> Why not one of us? They asked more than once. Not always a pleasant experience. When I returned to Limburg, I saw the same attitude towards outsiders. That alarms me … Limburg must change if it wants to grow up; it has to emancipate, become more tolerant … Aspects which you can point out in *Othello* as well. (Hermans, 2015b)

Although he indicated later on that his theatre company did not aim at doing political theatre and that *Othello* was mainly the most beautiful love story in the world, Hermans also argued that the outsider and its present-day relevance was an important side-line in his production.

Reviewers of the production too focused more than before on the relation to problems in Dutch multicultural society in comparing Iago's 'inexhaustible, abusive verbiage against coloured people (and women) to the verbal diarrhoea that Wilders [political leader of the PVV] emits on Muslims' (Prop, 2015). Another reviewer spoke of a 'gulf of indignation that went through the open-air theatre' during the use of terms such as *nikker* (Freriks, 2015). Both comments, however, were not only in the minority, but were also generally more related to the translation and less to the production as a whole. Moreover, they created a moral distance between Iago's actions and words and the position of the audience, thereby avoiding any need for critical self-reflection.

Despite the translator's intent, this *Othello* was generally hailed as an entertaining production, focusing on the love story and jealousy rather than on institutional racism or Black Pete (Aerts, 2015; Boegman, 2015; Devens, 2015; Veraart, 2015). Likewise, audience reaction, as seen in letters to the theatre company (*Publieksreacties*, 2019) or referred to in reviews, considered the production an enjoyable night in the open air, accompanied by some fine music (arias from Verdi's *Otello*). In contrast to the aforementioned indignation at the term *nikker*, the production provoked far more often furtive laughter during some of the derogatory terms used for Othello, a reaction Willems had not intended (Devens, 2015). A couple of months before this translation of *Othello* premiered in the hometown, Maastricht, the organisation of the Saint Nicholas festival in Maastricht stated that Black Pete would remain black (Gybels, 2014). A year later, Black Pete was still unquestioningly black in Maastricht (Hendrikx, 2015). The latest arrival of Saint Nicholas in the province of Maastricht in the winter of 2019 was still dominated in most places by the continuation of the Black Pete tradition, although some towns had terminated the use of red lips, earrings and curly hair, instead using 'sleek hair or Elvis haircuts' (Editorial, 2019). Not until 2018 would the first *Othello* in the Netherlands directly intervene in the racial discourse and blackface traditions. Before discussing that production and its impact, four Dutch fringe productions which started to veer away from the tradition of a white actor and the ambivalent response to this are analysed.

4 Movement from the Fringe: Ignorance, Indifference and Indignation

The tradition of blackface, discredited decades before in many other countries, lasted seemingly undisturbed well into the twenty-first century in the

Netherlands. The prominent *Othello* productions made use of white actors while alternating between the use of blackface, brownface, a black mask or no make-up at all. While these and other productions increasingly explored issues pertaining to ethnicity, religion, politics and the outsider, both the productions and their reception seem to have shied away from racial issues and generally focused on the domestic love tragedy, jealousy and revenge. Within this context of white actor dominance and an absence of critical discourse on race or blackface, I take a closer look at the few (peripheral) productions that made use of a non-white actor: the 1980 production by theatre company Nijinsky, the 1998 production by Cosmic Theatre Company, the 2001 production by NNT and the 2013 production by Theatre Company Diever. Was there a difference in directorial intent compared to the standard Dutch *Othellos* which employed white actors? To what extent did these fringe productions interrogate standard practices on the Dutch stage, blackface as such or racial aspects in Dutch society? Did they influence production, reception and the broader debate in Dutch society on racism? These questions are explored in this section.

4.1 The First Deviation: Ignorance and Indifference

The first production in the Netherlands that deviated from using a white actor was the 1980 production by theatre company Nijinsky, a fringe group with a small budget. Considering that it was the first company to cast a non-white actor as Othello, one would expect this would draw attention in reception, and one reviewer did comment on Bart Kiene's skin colour:

> Where Bart Kiene, who plays Othello, originates from, I do not know. He is not European, his skin colour is too dark for that, but he is also smaller and far more slender than the 'Moors' – African *negers*, I suppose – which I have seen played by Dutch actors. (Ruiten, 1980)

The reviewer went on to argue that this set Kiene apart from the other actors and that his fear of being an outsider made him susceptible to Iago's words. It was not so much the difference in skin colour, however, rather the 'delicate frailty of his figure' which supposedly set him apart from the rest of the cast. Although this reviewer alone picked up on the different casting for Othello, the comments revealed ignorance and indifference to the topic at a time when casting decisions had already emerged as a theme of discussion in the USA and the UK. Other reviewers of the production paid no attention to the casting decision, although everyone agreed that Kiene was by far the best actor of the group. The general trend of all reviewers, including the one quoted earlier, was that the main focus of the production was that of a stylised tragedy of love and jealousy (Heddema, 1980; Ruiten, 1980; Vroom, 1980).

None of the reviewers demonstrated any awareness of the discourse going on about blackface and race in *Othello*, and neither were any references made to new immigrants in Dutch society. That the reviewer just cited admitted to not knowing Kiene's country of birth was illustrative of the general mood in Dutch society at the time, which was generally ignorant of other cultures or the possibility of prejudice and racism in Dutch society. Kiene was born in Batavia in the Dutch colony of Indonesia in 1947. Batavia was renamed Jakarta when Indonesia achieved independence on 27 December 1949, and it was proclaimed the official national capital of Indonesia. Kiene migrated with his parents to the Netherlands at a young age during one of the migration waves to the Netherlands from 1945 to 1960. They were the first significant group of visibly different immigrants in Dutch society. As mentioned earlier, the perception was that integration did not present any problems, but later other stories emerged, also from the perspective of children, which highlighted the difficulties of integrating into Dutch society for these families:

> When my father came to the Netherlands, he lost everything, status, a good job. He never complained, but as a child you notice it. And it tears your heart apart. All those proud men, they all made it over there, and they had to start from scratch over here. So, this integration may seem to have worked out well, to have been easy in your minds, but not in our minds. (Jurriëns, 2001: 48)

However, none of these experiences materialised in the production, and from the director's point of view too the focus was firmly on the universality of emotions in a tragedy of love rather than on exploring other issues. Director Arend Bulder employed a sober set in which all references to place and time had been removed. Further, the text also did not mention Venice or Cyprus at all, while its continued use of the verse form was also seen as reducing the sense of realism from the production. In their movements on stage, which were at times more gymnastic than natural, the actors also froze in their positions from time to time and generally refrained from expressing emotions (Heijer, 1980). The use of glass-made swords and a set where colours such as white, grey, red and pink dominated also helped to enhance a stylised, fairy tale–like context, in which the interaction between Othello, Desdemona, Iago, Emilia and Cassio was central. Likewise, the programme notes (Program, 1980) described the production as 'a play about mankind's jealousy of his own happiness', reflecting the universality and timelessness of the emotions it aimed at exploring.

The stylisation drew special attention in the reception of the production, and opinions were mixed. On one hand, the company was applauded for choosing this experimental approach to the play and going against the more emotional theatre tradition of *Othello*. It was generally considered a courageous step that allowed for a different approach to the play taken by a company with only limited financial resources (Ruiten, 1980; Scholten, 1980; Vroom, 1980). This 'different approach' had, however, nothing to do with casting decisions or with a change in the discourse that was explored, but everything with the stylised approach to the play. The focus in reviews was still firmly on jealousy and the love tragedy, and the main point of criticism was that the stylisation distracted somewhat from that focus and the 'essential contrast of almost all of Shakespeare's tragedies between irrational emotions – this is how Shakespeare views jealousy – and emotionless reason – in this play personified by the power-hungry Iago' (Scholten, 1980).

While one might argue about the redundant interpretation of the play, it did indicate a perception that the production deviated too much from what Shakespeare might have meant. In fact, the name Shakespeare was not even mentioned at all in the programme notes to the production, which was commented upon as a logical consequence of the directorial choice to deviate from tradition and provide this stylised and somewhat abstract and unemotional interpretation of the tragedy, as compared to following the standard approach (Ruiten, 1980).

Interestingly, one reviewer indirectly commented on the Dutch colonial history in Indonesia, as he characterised the jealousy in this production as 'the hidden force' (Heijer, 1980). This referred to a prominent novel in Dutch literature, *The Hidden Force* by Louis Couperus, which was largely situated on the Indonesian island of Java around 1900. In the novel, the Western and rational world of the Dutch was contrasted with the supposedly more mysterious world of the indigenous population of Java, whose mysterious 'hidden force' undermined and resisted the attempts at control by the colonisers. This reference to the colonial past, in combination with an actor who had migrated from Indonesia, might have resulted in an exploration of race and blackface, or of the Dutch history of colonialism and even the developing multicultural society. However, none of this happened in the production or its reception. Even though the production deviated for the first time in the twentieth century from the traditional white actor for Othello, this specific aspect turned out to be a non-event, both in the reception of this production and in the impact it had on the following productions of *Othello* in 1988, 1996 and 1997. These productions were back to business as usual.

4.2 OJ Othello: *Indignation and Institutional Racism*

The second fringe production to deviate from the traditional white actor, in 1998, was an adaptation of the play by Cosmic Theatre Company in Amsterdam, titled *OJ Othello*. It was a one-man show of 90 minutes by black American actor Frank Sheppard, born 1950, who had worked in the Netherlands from 1986 onwards after a career in the United States. In the production, directed by Maarten van Hinte, the tragic stories of Othello and O. J. Simpson became intertwined in an exploration of the motives of two black persons who had murdered their white wives. The artistic leader of Cosmic Theatre Company, John Leerdam, repeatedly argued that the similarities between the two were the basis for the production:

> They both have a career in a white society. In that society,
> they feel uncertain of themselves. They are both black men
> with white wives. They murder their wives. O. J. Simpson
> was acquitted, but he could have committed the murder.
> (Leerdam, 1998a)

> O. J. Simpson thought he had been fully accepted in white
> society on account of his fame, wealth and status. However,
> after the murder of Nicole, he found out he was mistaken.
> The question of whether or not he was innocent was ulti-
> mately just a separation between black and white. (Leerdam,
> 1998b)

The first line Sheppard spoke was 'I hate Othello', while on both sides of
the podium television screens broadcast fragments of the trial of O. J.
Simpson in 1995. It immediately set the tone of a production which was
an interior monologue of Sheppard, who alternated between the under-
privileged black youth and the wealthy American embraced by high white
society, but also between Othello and Iago. To the background of hip-
hop music, Sheppard also alternated his language between a ghetto-based
idiom and upper-class American and Shakespeare English. While some
reviewers criticised the complexity and argued it was hard to follow his
inner turmoil with so many contrasting personalities, others applauded the
convincing versatility and complexity of O. J. Simpson's mindset. The
production turned out to be a hit in Edinburgh, where it won a Fringe
First Award in 1998 (Hellman, 1998; Nightingale, 1998; Roodnat, 1998;
Van der Jagt, 1998). The director of Cosmic Theatre Company, John
Leerdam, indicated the importance of skin colour in the production but
also hinted at a specific relevance within Dutch society:

> [O. J. Simpson is] a complex man, who very much wants to
> be a white man, because that is his ideal. However, another
> voice inside his head tells him he should not and never can
> forget where he came from. Those two sides are in eternal
> conflict. Even though he does not want colour to play a role,

he finds out that it is important. That is his tragedy. Even more significant is the tragedy that he had been looking for a father's love, who was hardly ever there when he needed him. Many Surinam and Antillean fathers failed. Fathers need to learn and take responsibility. (Leerdam, 1998a)

John Leerdam would have known the problem first-hand, being born in Curaçao to a Surinam father and a mother from St. Kitts and having migrated to the Netherlands in 1982 to study at the Theatre School in Amsterdam. He worked with Cosmic Theatre Company from 1996 onwards and became the director and artistic leader in 1999. In 2003, he became a member of parliament for the Dutch Social Democratic Party; in 2006, he received the Lifetime Service Award of the Council for Opportunity in Education for his efforts in creating opportunities for immigrants. His references to Surinam and Antillean fathers reflected directly on the problematic integration of these two major ethnic groups in multicultural Dutch society. As indicated earlier, mass migration from these two former slave colonies of the Netherlands took place from the 1970s and 1980s onwards amidst worsening economic, social and political conditions in Surinam and the Netherlands Antilles. Research at the time of this production also saw the absence of a father figure as one of the causes for the poor integration of Antilleans, the relatively high criminality, school drop-out rates and unemployment figures among these migrant groups (de Jong, Masson & Steijlen, 1997; Van Hulst, 1997).

Leerdam used this production to not only reflect on racial discrimination or Dutch multicultural society in general, but also as a springboard to criticise the lack of black actors on the Dutch stage:

I have got a list of seventy-seven immigrant Dutch actors who would join my theatre company at any moment. But they do not get a job elsewhere. Why not? Because the theatre world is one of the most conservative in Dutch society. (Leerdam, 1998c)

In Leerdam's opinion, the Dutch theatre world was conservative and white in the extreme but steadfastly refused to acknowledge the fact, resulting in a continuation of the status quo:

> As an artistic director of a theatre company I, a black man, am still a rarity in the Netherlands. It is nonsense what they keep on repeating in this small theatre world: that black and white have long been perfectly integrated, and that therefore no special attention is required on that specific topic. (Leerdam, 1998a)

Where the 1980 production demonstrated a complete ignorance of or indifference to the racial discourse, *OJ Othello* highlighted it, demonstrating indignation both at the Dutch theatrical world and at the multicultural society and its ongoing institutional racism. It may perhaps be understandable that the reception of the performance in Edinburgh did not pick up on the 'new' approach this production brought to *Othello* in the Netherlands. The main attention was more by way of its positioning in the O. J. debate, the provocation and complexity of using one person to present multiple perspectives, the lack of coherence, the multimedia approach and on trampling Shakespeare's verse (Bassett, 2000; Gardner, 1998; McMillan, 1998; Nightingale, 1998). The production's focus on a racial discourse or the use of a black actor was, after all, not new to British theatre or critics. In contrast to reviews of productions from countries that are supposedly culturally more different, there would arguably have been no clear necessity for supposing, let alone exploring, a possibly different background in the case of a Dutch production.

On the other hand, one would have expected Dutch reception to the production to address these issues. However, reception of the production paid hardly any attention to the topics Leerdam raised, and themes such as blackface, the casting of Othello, multicultural society or institutional racism were notably absent from the reviews, which mainly focused on O. J. Simpson rather than engaging in a critical discourse on Dutch society or theatre (Hellman, 1998; Roodnat, 1998; Van der Jagt, 1998). In 2015, Leerdam would stage another fringe production in Amsterdam, *Race* by David Mamet. At the same time, the farewell tour of Van Hove's *Othello* was playing in the main theatre of Amsterdam. Although Leerdam's production received no major newspaper reviews, Schaap, who was also a theatre correspondent for national newspapers, compared the two productions in an online cultural blog:

> Hans Kesting is playing this 'black' role, because directors and media consider the white Hans Kesting to be the best actor for the role. Herdigein [a Dutch actor working with Leerdam] is a black actor playing a black character. Also, because he best fits the role. The two productions in Amsterdam indicate the intense divide in the Dutch cultural world. In our main theatre, a well-educated and mainly white audience watches a white actor playing a black character, while everything in the program notes wants to make Othello colourless. It is still considered normal in the Netherlands that our main theatre company hardly selects actors that are not white. (Schaap, 2015)

Almost two decades after Leerdam's call for more diversity, the pattern did not seem to have changed.

4.3 Black Comedy: Ignoring Race

The next production which featured a black actor as Othello was a 2001 production directed by Koos Terpstra for NNT, a regional company in the north-east of the Netherlands. The actor who played Othello was Eric van Sauers, a stand-up comedian with a Dutch mother and a Surinam father. The production opened with Iago on stage saying, 'I hate that *neger*! I hate that *neger*!' in a deviation from the translation used by Bert Voeten. It could have set the tone for this production, and the actor playing Iago referred to a break with the traditional approach to the play:

> I think that it is a good thing that a *neger* plays Othello, because up to now he is repeatedly being played by a white man with black make-up. (Hoogmartens, 2001)

Although Hoogmartens was not entirely correct as Othello had also been played by a white actor without blackface in 1993, his reasoning that it was a relatively new approach was justified, although it also indicated ignorance regarding the situation in anglophone countries, where the tradition had long been abolished. In reception, only one reviewer commented specifically on the relation between skin colour and casting decision, arguing that it was 'obvious that Terpstra asked [Van Sauers] for Othello, because he has a dark skin colour' (Van der Laan, 2001). Although up to now it was far from obvious in the Netherlands, Van Sauers himself indicated that it presented no problem for him that his skin colour might have influenced the director's choice: 'Suppose a casting agency should ask me for a role of bank robber. Should I refuse that role? Yeah, fuck you, man!' (Van Sauers, 2001). The outspoken comments indicated a tendency to cast actors like Van Sauers for specific roles, which were echoed by similar remarks from *OJ Othello* director Leerdam: 'A young actor like Gustav Borreman, who is black, but born and bred in this country, wants to be judged on his acting skills . . . He says: "I did the Theatre Academy, I speak Dutch fluently, but I only get cast for certain roles. The cleaner, the migrant worker or some foreigner"' (Leerdam, 1998c). Although comments such as these might have been the starting point for further debate, the main attention regarding casting decisions for this *Othello* was fully focused on Van Sauers' cabaret background.

The rest of the production and its reception also indicated how little impact the 1998 Leerdam production had had on the Dutch staging of *Othello*. Apart from briefly referring to Van Sauers in terms such as 'black actor' (Schaap, 2001) or 'relaxed *neger*' (Langen, 2001), skin colour, blackface or racism hardly played a role in the production or its reception. This *Othello* was firmly centred on the topics of jealousy, love, treason and revenge. Van Sauers himself also argued that this was a play about the universal emotions of a man and that it was the intent to turn Othello into 'just an ordinary, recognisable man' (Van Sauers, 2001). Terpstra's choice of Van Sauers was largely motivated by the fact that the actor had been a stand-up comedian, as Terpstra intended to add more humour to *Othello*: 'Why should I not liven up *Othello* with some lame jokes? Shakespeare himself did the same. I refuse to accept that everything must be so profoundly serious, the way the theatre police wants it to be. I am in for everything' (Terpstra, 2001a). As a director, Terpstra himself was already known for his approach in breaking the borders between cabaret and theatre, which he considered the best method:

> Shakespeare did it all. His plays contained jokes, songs were sung, there was dancing. But then they took Shakespeare apart. The jokes became cabaret, the songs musical. All that was left for Shakespeare was theatre ... I want to bring it back together again. That is fun theatre for a broad audience. With jokes. But that is suspicious, because subsidized theatre seems to think that funny plays are not allowed. (Terpstra, 2001b)

The humour and cabaret style were portrayed in many different forms: in a parody of a whole series of Dutch lager advertisements as a means of visualising Cassio getting drunk, in a message from the battlefield being delivered by a downpour of fake homing pigeons, in the arrival in port being announced by a group of actors blowing in glasses to imitate the sound of the sea, in magic tricks on stage with a disappearing handkerchief and also in the very clothes, which were a mishmash of colours and styles. Othello, for example, wore a bright orange pair of trousers, later covered with bearskin around his legs.

With so much attention focused on cabaret and humour, one would expect reception to focus on this as well, which it did, although not always in an entirely positive manner. While all reviewers applauded the introduction of humour in the play, most of them saw an imbalance between comic and cabaret-style elements and the tragic core of the play, and the term 'soap' was frequently used in reviews (Bots, 2001; Buijs, 2001; Freriks, 2001; Langen, 2001; Strien, 2001; Vervoort, 2001). They also focused on the traditional tragedy of love, jealousy and miscommunication, which might have been more prominently present. While the 'theatre police' criticised Terpstra's *Othello* on this aspect, they also ignored any discourse on racial topics, with only the odd reviewer commenting in general terms on immigrants and the rise of populist parties (Van der Laan, 2001).

Online reviews written by audience members were mainly positive but exclusively focused on the humour and fun of the production, while simultaneously indicating that regularly small numbers of 'serious Shakespeare lovers left the theatre screaming in despair' (Moose, 2001). The production had started as a small-scale fringe *Othello*, intended only for a couple of performances in the home theatre of the company in the provincial town of Groningen. However, despite the mixed reviews, it grew into a production that would tour the country for ten weeks. Its popularity, however, did not result in another approach to blackface, race or casting decisions in *Othello*. After the interruption and indignity of *OJ Othello* in 1998, it would be back to business as usual in *Othello* and the next three main theatre productions on the Dutch stage in 2003, 2006 and 2012, once again employed white actors as Othello, with or without blackface.

4.4 Othello *in the Forest: The Green-Eyed Monster*

After the traditional white actor's casting, with or without blackface, in the preceding decade, in 2013, a fourth production by Theatre Company Diever deviated again from the traditional white actor. Theatre Company Diever is not one of the main, subsidised theatre companies in the Netherlands, but can best be described as a semi-professional company building largely upon a local amateur cast. The company does not tour the country, but plays in its open-air theatre in the forest next to the small town of Diever, averaging some 2,500 inhabitants and located far away from the major cities. However, it has staged, since 1946, one major open-air Shakespeare production every year and has become an important Shakespeare tradition in the Netherlands, drawing an average yearly audience of around 20,000, including five royal visits so far. In 2016, the company built a small, Globe-like theatre, allowing it to stage productions in winter as well. The director, Jack Nieborg, argued that his choice for a black actor was a conscious one:

> I absolutely did not want an Othello with charcoal on his
> cheeks and a Drenthe [the Dutch province where the play
> was staged] accent. I had a tip about Malcolm, a twenty-
> year-old kid from Saint Marten [a former Dutch Caribbean

colony], who had moved to the Netherlands two years ago
... Over there he only spoke English. It is a miracle he
managed the Dutch text ... I did want the 'we' in his
pronunciation to be 'oowee'. I like that. He had to be
different. (Nieborg, 2013a)

In this ambivalent observation, Nieborg indicated that on one hand, he
wanted to steer away from the blackface tradition, thus he chose a
Caribbean actor for the role; however, on the other hand, he differentiated
him further by exaggerating his accent, a tradition also employed in blackface theatre and minstrelsy that enhanced the stereotypical presentation of
black persons. It served to highlight the ignorance or indifference to the
sensitivity of the topic, and despite Nieborg's conscious choice of actor, the
racial topic as such did not enter the production. The posters advertising
the production showed an Othello with green make-up as the colour of
jealousy, the audience magazine showed photos of green make-up being
applied on Othello (although he played without make-up), and in
audience reaction, it was remarked that one had expected a green
Othello ('Othello', 2013; Terdu, 2013). The advertisement for the
production played on the same topic:

> Othello is green with jealousy. And likewise, *The Tragedy of*
> *Othello, the Moor of Venice* contains powerful emotions:
> revenge, love, honour and heartache. (*De Gids*, 2013)

The same green colour also recurred in Othello's costume, which had a
green lining that became more and more visible in the course of the
production. In the audience magazine, the colophon was printed on a
green background, while other pages showed a white background with
many words printed in green. In the same section, a summary of the play
and a comment by Nieborg never once referred to race, but fully concen-
trated on the topic of jealousy ('Othello', 2013). Finally, the book which
contained the used translation consisted of a green front and back cover; this
translation was by Nieborg himself and a far cry from the brutal translations
used by Van Hove (Bouazza, 2003) or Hermans (Willems, 2015). It lacked

any modern-day racial slurs, while Nieborg had even deleted many of the explicit racial or ethnic references in the play. The Duke's line 'Your son-in-law is far more fair than black' (1.3.291) was, for example, removed in the translation; also, Othello's lines in the final speech on 'Where a malignant and a turbaned Turk/Beat a Venetian and traduced the state,/I took him by th' throat the circumcised dog/And smote him – thus!' (5.2.351–4) were also removed in the translation (Nieborg, 2013b: 18, 87).

This production appeared decades after not only the anglophone countries had stopped using blackface and introduced racism as a topic, but also neighbouring Germany had repeatedly and controversially started reapplying make-up to further interrogate blackface and racism. The focus on green and the use of green make-up might have made for an interesting and relatively easy perspective to introduce the practice of blackface or the topic of racism. Underneath the first more superficial layer of green make-up, indicating jealousy, a second deeper and more meaningful layer of skin colour might have been revealed, possibly indicating more real and underlying discriminating patterns. However, this did not happen, and the reception also duly focused on jealousy and revenge while the choice of the Caribbean actor, his accent or race as such never entered the reviews (Freriks, 2013; Janssen, 2013; Kleuver, 2013; Nederkoorn, 2013; Rings, 2013; Van Ruiten, 2013). The only reviewer to comment on blackface and racism referred to the Dutch tradition of Black Pete and its 'supposedly racist trait', while admitting that the tradition had been modelled on slavery practices and might be unacceptable for people outside the Netherlands. He also argued that 'children, also coloured ones, from the Netherlands and from abroad, unconditionally accept Saint Nicholas and Black Pete' (Jansen, 2013). Three years later, as discussed earlier in a Dutch context, an investigation by the national Dutch ombudsperson for children made explicit how the character of Black Pete contributed to bullying, exclusion and discrimination of coloured children.

Where the aforementioned 2001 NNT production was criticised for veering off too much into a ludicrous, cabaret-style *Othello*, the production in Diever was considered to maintain a proper balance between tragedy and comedy, in line with the tradition of Theatre Company Diever. On one hand, easy jocular laughter was introduced, for example in Nieborg's translation of the first lines of scene 3.4, where Desdemona asked a servant where Cassio was 'hanging out', to which the servant replied, 'Where he is usually hanging out.' To Desdemona's exasperated question where Othello was 'usually hanging out', the servant replied, 'He's usually hanging out of his pants' (Nieborg, 2013b: 50). Reviewers applauded the introduction of these 'cheeky little dialogues' as perfectly balanced and in line with the Diever tradition:

> Director Jack Nieborg has adapted, translated and lightened up Shakespeare's tragedy about jealousy and revenge. It fits the Diever tradition, where well-attended Shakespeare productions are yearly staged, and where the more serious plays are not performed too morbidly. That does not take away from the fact that Nieborg usually manages to achieve a proper balance between earnestness and humour. (Janssen, 2013)

It was the second time the company had taken on *Othello* and reviewers looked duly back on its earlier production:

> According to critics, back then [in 1989] the production was all about jealousy and passion. A quarter of a century later, under the direction of Jack Nieborg, it's about jealousy, passion, loyalty, power, envy and revenge – just a little bit more. (Van Ruiten, 2013)

The brief recapitulation of the 1989 *Othello* was not entirely accurate as the focus was not only on jealousy and passion, but also on the struggle for power and the ability to 'manipulate innocent people into repulsive acts in order to gain revenge' (ter Horst-Rep, 1989). However, what was more interesting was that twenty-four years later, the reception continued to focus on the feelings and universal emotions, irrespective of any racial discourse. Neither the evolvement of multicultural society nor the introduction of a Caribbean actor seemed to influence the reception of the play.

Considering these four peripheral productions that deviated from the Dutch tradition of using white actors for the title role, one might have expected them to at least initiate a debate on blackface or racism or perhaps only to result in reception that focused on these topics. However, this was not the case, neither in production nor in reception, with the exception perhaps of the 1998 *OJ Othello*. However, in *OJ Othello*, both its vision and reception were mixed, and the topics it did introduce were quickly forgotten in the productions that followed. The debates on race and acting, race and *Othello*, actors in blackface, the use of white actors in *Othello*, Black Pete and the dilemmas *Othello* presented in exploring race did not seem to have been picked up in the Netherlands. Next, the author discusses the 2018 *Othello* and its rerun in 2020, the first main house production that introduced a black actor for the title role and tried to initiate a debate on blackface and race.

5 Othello Is Black and That Matters

'Othello is black and that matters' (Janssens, 2018) was the headline of one of the reviews of the first main house production of *Othello* in the Netherlands with a black actor. It seemed an odd headline, considering the anglophone or the German performance history of the play, but in the Netherlands, the production by Het Nationale Toneel (the National Theatre) turned out to be a revelation. In the following section, the production, its casting decisions, the set, the use of stage directions, its focus on institutional racism, its highly enthusiastic yet also problematic reception, its relation to the discourse on blackface and race in the Dutch theatre world and Dutch society as well as its potential effects are discussed. The author rounds this off by considering the 2020 rerun of the popular production, this time no longer confined to the smaller theatre auditoriums but playing in all the big auditoriums throughout the country.

5.1 Casting Decisions and Race

When asked about her choice of actor for Othello, director Daria Bukvić mentioned how absurd it was that in the Netherlands a major company had never used a black actor for Othello. On one hand, she compared herself to Othello as an outsider in Dutch society: 'I have been addressed as a foreigner all my life. In a way, I am Othello too, but I am white' (Bukvić, 2018a). However, Bukvić, a political refugee from Bosnia, aimed at moving beyond the traditional outsider theme of previous Dutch *Othellos* and wanted to address race. When asked about the choice of a black actor, she argued that it was essential to the role because you 'cannot act institutional racism', referring both to the play as such and to the specific context of Dutch society: 'All characters have the usual human traits, such as jealousy, fear, anger. But Othello is accredited with traits because of his colour. That is institutional racism. A white person would not be affected by that. When Baudet [leader of the populist party FVD] says something, you never hear: "Oh, that white man again." It is a form of racism that is deep in the nerves of this play and this society' (Bukvić, 2018b). In a discussion on previous *Othello* productions in the Netherlands, both the director and the actor playing Othello, Werner Kolf, reflected on the general trend in Dutch performance history and how their production compared to that, but also on the pushback they got for choosing a 'new' approach:

> What is particularly important, and what has been ignored too much, is that a successful, black man has an affair with a white woman, and suddenly all white characters are opposed to this man. You should not ignore that, and the best way to demonstrate it, is by using a black actor. If you use a white actor, it will never come across so well. (Kolf, 2020)

> In 2018, when the production premiered, there were so many people, actors of other main companies, who thought it was disgusting that I saw racism as the main theme of the play. They told me I was misleading the audience. (Bukvić, 2020)

When asked to what extent other Dutch companies had seen it as a play about jealousy and love, Bukvić mentioned that this had been the general approach so far, and that 'whenever they included discrimination, it was mainly focused on the outsider in general, rather than on racial issues' (Bukvić, 2020). When queried further on previous productions, Kolf was also quite outspoken:

> Their approach does not respect the play and our society. Yes, I
> saw the Van Hove production [the 2012 rerun in which Kesting
> played Othello without make-up] several years ago, and it does
> not do justice to the play or to Othello. You see Othello doing a
> brief prayer to Allah, and thus they have shown that Othello is
> not a white man. With all due respect, but it is this white way of
> thinking how to stage this play and how that is the only way. Of
> course, people should be free to choose their interpretation, like
> Theatre Company Maastricht also did [the 2015 production
> with Koen de Sutter as a white Othello], but I am not going
> there, I cannot take it. I think you can tell the story better with a
> black actor. (Kolf, 2020)

The divide in the Dutch theatre world was made quite explicit and Kolf saw
this as a reflection of how black actors were looked at in the theatre world
and a wider Dutch context, echoing many of the statements made two
decades ago by Leerdam (director of *OJ Othello*): 'Othello is a man who
loves his wife very much, who'd give his life for her, but who is misguided
into thinking her unfaithful. But when you consider all that is happening to
him, then that is, indeed, exactly how things work in the world; in the world
of theatre, and also in the street' (Kolf, 2020). In a similar vein, Bukvić
argued how the play could not achieve its full potential and would be
'avoiding the issue' with a white actor while making short shrift of the
argument that there were not enough black actors, just as Leerdam did
twenty years ago:

> Come on, you cannot mean that. No, it is unwillingness.
> They don't think it is important enough. Kolf is an incred-
> ibly good actor and he is black. Therefore, he brings some-
> thing extra: the pain of a black man. Not every black
> character needs a black actor, but it does if the role is
> about racial grief, about what it is to be black or white.
> Othello speaks about being sold as a slave, about his jour-
> ney. With our colonial past, how can we let those words be
> spoken by a white man? (Bukvić, 2018a)

While arguments such as these might sound outdated in the anglophone world, where the debate on colour-conscious casting has been more prominent, they were still relatively unexplored in Dutch society and theatre, as demonstrated earlier. Within the context of perceived institutional racism in the Dutch theatre world and Dutch society at large and the increasingly vehement debate about blackface traditions with problematic racist undertones, both Bukvić and Kolf considered it imperative to adhere to naturalistic casting, as doing otherwise would to them be pretending to live in a world where racism did not exist. Other actors of the company also revealed having spoken a lot about racism in the play and in society, and shared that the director had told them they had to read *Hallo Witte Mensen* [*Hello White People*] (Nzume, 2017a), a book on institutional racism in Dutch society. On having read this book, one of the actors, Nieuwerf (2018), said, 'We have grown convinced of the importance of this focus. We consider ourselves to be open-minded, non-racist persons. But now we are finding out, and this is confrontational, that we ourselves are part of a racist system.' While it indicated the focus of the production and actors, his remarks were also a reminder of the previous lack of awareness on the topic.

5.2 Black and White in the Production

Othello's isolation and the aspect of institutional racism that seeped through the pores of Venetian society in this production was strengthened not only because all the other actors were white, but also because they were white in the extreme. Their trousers, shirts, dresses, pyjamas and even socks and shoes were all white. They also wore white wigs and their skin too had been whitened up further with make-up (Figure 1). Bukvić indicated that this differentiated Othello in colour and that she also aimed at referring to the excesses of racial discourse, looking for 'a kind of aesthetically berserk image' (Bukvić, 2018b), which was to be perpetrated in not only the extreme forms of propaganda, but also in other media:

> We are referring to the Aryan Empire, Leni Riefenstahl [a German filmmaker and photographer who worked for the Nazis], *Lord of the Rings*, *The Hunger Games*, those kinds of

Figure 1 White in the extreme – Cassio, Emilia, Desdemona
and Iago ©*Sanne Peper*

aesthetics, blue eyes, white elves, white hair. Werner's head
and hands are the only element of colour in the production.
The lack of colour in this world is a symbolically extreme
expression of the ruling elite, extremely white. (Bukvić, 2020)

The similarity in clothing and make-up also had the effect of partly
negating the differentiation between the white actors in the production,
who converged at times from what were individual human beings into an
indistinguishable group, identified only by colour. This was reinforced
immediately from the start of the production: Othello and Desdemona
danced frontstage and all the other characters stood in the background
next to each other, presenting one indistinguishable, white supremacist
front while singing together in a slow, Gregorian manner. The song was
a choir adaptation resembling the melancholy chanson 'Tomorrow Is My
Turn', Nina Simone's English version of Aznavour's 'L'amour, c'est

comme un jour'. The choir music and the sound design of the production added to an inescapable and preordained sense of doom from the start, and the composer, Wilko Sterke (2020), argued that his music would create the effect of 'being very slowly sucked into a tunnel'. As the choir slowly sang the deeply sad and repetitive lines, the reference to the inevitability of doom and the dominance of colour found expression in the following lines: 'White angels singing/It's my turn/It's my turn/It's my turn'. The dress and the uniformity led to easy associations with the Ku Klux Klan and how exclusion, isolation and marginalisation could easily lead to merciless racial violence. The set too contributed to the idea of a white trap with its inverse V-like shape and large pieces of white cloth on both sides, resembling some form of a white tunnel towards which one was inevitably drawn and ultimately trapped inside.

A reflecting mirror floor enhanced the effect of whiteness and the only element of colour in this world was Othello's. Although he was also dressed in white clothes, indicating a sense of similarity with the world around him, his skin colour distinctly set him apart. As the only visible differentiation were his hands and his head, they seemed to form an almost disembodied part of his persona. It presented the image of a man who had achieved a degree of whiteness and acceptance but who would always stand out, caught in a world of contrasting forces and not at home in either one of them (Figure 2). The idea of the mirror floor, however, extended beyond enhancing the colours, as Bukvić argued that it was also meant as a confrontation, originating from the previously mentioned book *Hello White People*, wherein the author held up a mirror to white people about institutional racism: 'There is a tendency in society now to interrogate, as white people, our seemingly ingrained behaviour which has its roots in our colonial past. In addition, the mirror also reflects the waters of the Mediterranean, now Europe's largest coffin with all the refugees who are dying there' (Bukvić, 2018b). The directorial intent and references, in this case, seemed perhaps too complex and multilayered for an audience to take in all at once. None of the reviewers commented on it, but the strong visual effect the mirror floor had in highlighting the white colour and isolating Othello in this white world was unmistakable.

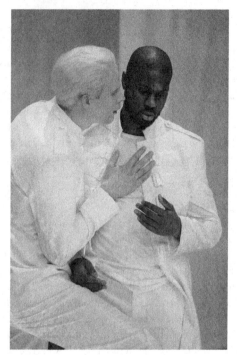

Figure 2 Black and white – Iago and Othello ©*Sanne Peper*

5.3 Physical Abuse, Racism and Perception

An intriguing aspect of the production was the use of stage directions which indicated physical abuse from Othello towards Desdemona. When the stage direction read 'Striking her' (4.1.239), Dutch productions tended to have Othello physically strike Desdemona. Although the harshness of the strike varied, it would always indicate a troubling aspect of Othello's character – hitting an innocent woman. In this production, Iago spoke the stage direction out loud: 'Othello hits Desdemona', followed by silence on the stage. Next, Iago said, 'Now, now, now, now', and repeated the stage direction 'Othello hits Desdemona', after which he and Lodovico reacted in a horrified manner at Othello's supposedly violent behaviour. However, although Iago had said the stage direction twice, the action did not actually take place on stage. This had a double effect: on the hand, it removed the troubling image of Othello lashing out at Desdemona and enhanced the concept that even the idea of a violent act by Othello was not only indirectly, but also directly prompted by Iago. On the other hand, and far more interesting, was the underlying concept that Othello's supposedly violent nature existed only in the minds of the white characters rather than in reality. It indicated that racism created not only stereotypes, but also white people's perception of black people's actions, irrespective of whether they had actually taken place. Preconceived notions would not only influence, but also take the place of reality. A few lines later, at the end of the scene, Lodovico said, 'I am sorry that I am deceived in him' (4.1.282), to which the following line was added: 'A savage will always be a savage' (Duysker, 2017: 83). This indicated how Othello would always be judged according to pre-existing stereotypes, regardless of whether he hit Desdemona, which turned into irrelevance as the stereotype was fixed and would always win out over reality.

A final stage direction indicating violence from Othello towards Desdemona can be found near the end of the play, indicating the murder of Desdemona: '[He] smothers her' (5.2.83). Here the deviation in the Bukvić production was even more substantial. First, in an almost ritual-like scene, Desdemona's bed, covered with white satin, was carried to the front of the stage by the white actors. On the bed, Desdemona lay down in white lingerie, calling for Othello to join her while all the white actors lined up to watch what would happen. The scene radiated a sense of someone being ritually led to the slaughter, except that Othello was the real victim. He sat down next to her bed, visibly furious and desperate, but he did not lift a finger. When one would have expected Othello to smother Desdemona as per the original stage direction, there was instead a long silence, after which Iago entered and spoke, by way of stage direction, 'Othello murders Desdemona'. After another moment of silence, Roderigo entered and repeated 'Othello murders Desdemona'. Next, one after the other, Lodovico, Bianca, Emilia and Cassio did the same. They concluded their stage directions of what supposedly had happened by reverting to a choir-like Gregorian chant, resembling the beginning of the production. The convergence that was already visible from the start of the production, between the white characters on stage, reached its crescendo at the end. From individual human beings, they morphed into a homogeneous, murderous group with a single, race-driven perception of reality. Even Emilia, Desdemona's confidante, was unable to withstand the lure and the perception of the group as she lashed out verbally at Othello, referring to him as a '*neger*' and 'stupid ape' (Duysker, 2017: 101, 102).

However, just as Othello in this production had never hit Desdemona, he did not kill her at the end, and several times during this scene, Desdemona tried to convince other characters that she was not dead, urging them to 'stop. This has to stop now' (Duysker, 2017: 101). However, Desdemona's words did not register with the other characters, not even her direct reply to Emilia's lines that she was lying murdered in her bed: 'What are you talking about, I am sitting right here!' (Duysker, 2017: 102) (Figure 3). The other characters fully ignored reality in a scene which made for uncomfortable viewing but arguably also tackled one of the 'problems' of the possibly racist aspects of the play: Othello

Figure 3 Racism decrees reality: the 'death' of Desdemona – Emilia and Desdemona ©*Sanne Peper*

might be a dignified Moor in the play or any given production, he might be corrupted by a totally convincing Iago and helpless and almost without guilt, but he did hit Desdemona, he did kill her in the end, and in the text of the play, he did say that he reverted to his original nature. By putting the stage directions into Iago's, Lodovico's, Emilia's and the other characters' mouths, Othello might be naive, he might be duped by Iago, he might be inclined towards jealousy, but he did not resort to violence. It strengthened the idea of institutional racism in a literally white world that wanted to see a black man only as a murderer. The deviation, Bukvić argued, was necessary:

> That Othello murders Desdemona is what the racist, white person would like to see. In 2018 we need to break with the expectation that Othello, after four hundred years, is still required to do exactly the same. Othello has been caught for four hundred years in that stereotypical ending, which is why we are changing it. (Bukvić, 2018a)

From a meta-theatrical perspective, one might argue that when the other actors saw that Othello did not adhere to the stage directions in the original text, they admonished him verbally to get back into his four hundred-year-old role. These deviations also cut into the argument of Hugh Quarshie, discussed earlier, about whether it was still ethical for a black person to take on the role as it risked reinforcing existing stereotypes. The changes made in this production, particularly in the fifth act, might have addressed that problem and, according to Bukvić, done justice to the fact that 'Shakespeare wrote an anti-racist play, but time has overtaken the play in a way that the fifth act becomes highly problematic today' (Bukvić, 2020). This might be a challenge for main house anglophone productions too, which generally tend to be more respectful towards the original script.

The changes continued after the perceived death of Desdemona, as the stage direction 'He stabs himself' (5.2.354) was changed into a line spoken by Iago: 'Othello picks up his weapon and kills himself' (Duysker, 2017: 104). That too, however, was never a reality in this production, and after Desdemona's plea to Othello – 'Don't you dare' (Duysker, 2017: 104) – a quick sequence of events took place on stage. Iago snatched one of the white cloths from the bed and tied it around Othello's neck. Desdemona tried to run towards the scene but was prevented by Rodrigo, while all the other characters slowly walked away from the scene of the murder, not wanting anything to do with the crime. Othello did not murder Desdemona, she was alive; however, racism decreed another reality. White society wanted the Othello who murdered Desdemona, so this became the reality and what had happened. After Othello's murder, Emilia sang the classic protest song 'Strange Fruit', which protested racism and the lynching of African Americans: 'Black bodies swinging in the southern breeze / Strange fruit hanging from the poplar trees'. It was a forceful reminder of how the past had become the present. For Bukvić, the production was all about present-day issues which still dominate Dutch society, and *Othello* by Shakespeare was the perfect tool to reach a large audience:

> Shakespeare shows how Othello is a victim of his environ-
> ment. But he also turns him into a murderer. Because of
> unfaithfulness, a kind of King Kong who breaks the neck of
> the white girl: this is another stereotype, which influences
> how we look at the black man . . . It is painful actually that
> this four hundred-year-old story is still relevant today. I
> could have written a text on the topic, but Shakespeare
> draws a larger audience. People turned Shakespeare into a
> holy grail. I use that grail to seduce them to come and watch
> a production that tells a relevant story. (Bukvić, 2018a)

Another aspect that aroused debate was Othello's supposed victimisation at the end of the production, discussed earlier. In this context, it is interesting to consider the reaction of one of the main participants in the debate on Dutch racism, Gloria Wekker, who authored the study *White Innocence* (2016). She criticised the ending for making Othello too much of a victim and would have preferred a more powerful Othello. In the end, she argued, we are still watching the subjugation of a black man (Wekker, 2018). A similar argument was picked up by the reviewer of the Christian newspaper *Trouw* (one of the few voices to challenge, albeit tentatively, the lack of a black Othello in the past), who argued that the end forced Othello too much into the role of a victim (Van der Kooi, 2018). This victimisation was further picked up on in newspapers and journals; *Volkskrant*, the left-wing newspaper of the Netherlands, joined the debate a week later by arguing the contrary: the very act of making Othello a victim helped to make explicit 'racism and its poisonous effects' (Wensink, 2018). Bukvić, on the other hand, argued that 'Othello is of course not a stable, cosy man. If he would only be a victim, a faultless victim, that is even more racist and moralistic, and unrealistic too' (Bukvić, 2018c).

The production ended with Othello asking the characters on stage, 'Are you afraid of me?' Next, standing centre stage by himself, he moved towards the audience, breaking down the fourth wall and, addressing them directly, repeated the question: 'Are you afraid of me?' (Duysker, 2017: 104). As part of the theatre code, one was not supposed to answer the question of an actor on stage; however, not reacting also implicated guilt as it forced the audience uncomfortably into the role of the fearful, silent majority. This was a brutal and confrontational *Othello*, which for the first time in a main house production in the Netherlands since the 1863 Ira Aldridge version had not only put a black actor on stage, but had also rediscovered racism as the core element of *Othello*, something hitherto unseen in the Netherlands.

5.4 Ambivalent Reception and Aftermath

The reception of the production was generally enthusiastic. It sold out, and reviewers agreed that it was squarely about racism, although some argued that the dichotomy was perhaps somewhat too black and white. However, most people complimented the production's focus on racism. The general argument was that this *Othello* brought the debate on racism to the heart of the Dutch stage and society and showed how irrational fear and prejudice determined perception: 'It makes *Othello* inescapable. In the Netherlands of today, with all the debates about identity, this *Othello* is necessary' (Freriks, 2018). Reviewers noted how the production had moved away from a play about revenge and jealousy to a play about a black man's inevitable conviction in a white man's world: 'Werner Kolf, exclusively based on skin colour, falls by definition out of the group. That is an uncomfortable realisation, which you cannot avoid as an audience' (Janssens,

2018). However, not all reviewers concurred, and some lamented the move to change Othello from a tragic hero to a 'one-dimensional victim' (Brans, 2018). However, these were only some exceptions as most reviewers were enthusiastic about the production, using terms such as 'convincing', 'powerful', 'remarkable', 'impressive' and 'exemplary' (de Jong, 2018; Freriks, 2018; Hoogendoorn, 2018; Janssen, 2018; Janssens, 2018).

However, the 'uncomfortable truths' and (institutional) racism that dominated reception of the production seemed to be reserved in reviews for 'others' in the Dutch society, which a reviewer succinctly summarised in arguing that this '*Othello* is about the power of the disgruntled, dissatisfied, white lower-class man' (Van der Kooi, 2018). The mirror Bukvić intended to uphold seemed to be limited to specific groups in Dutch society, which was also exemplified by the way Iago was reviewed. During the production, he once replied to one of Othello's commands with 'At your service' (Duysker, 2017: 62), citing a popular phrase by Pim Fortuyn, while also imitating his soldier-like salute. Fortuyn was a prominent leader of the right-wing populist party Lijst Pim Fortuyn; he was murdered in 2002, resulting in an almost martyr-like status and a strong move towards the right in Dutch politics. Reviewers argued how the reference to Fortuyn made Iago even less sympathetic and that it installed a useful link in the production to the Dutch context:

> Iago is evil incarnate ... and the well-known Fortuyn
> gesture draws the play into the present. They are people
> such as Iago and Fortuyn, the people of 'I don't discriminate
> but ... ' who, out of self-interest, want to perpetuate the fear
> of all that is different from the white masses. (de Jong, 2018)

Similar references in reviews were made to Dutch politician Geert Wilders, who heads the populist party PVV, following in the footsteps of Pim Fortuyn (Hoogendoorn, 2018). The actors' white wigs were compared to Wilders' hair, which used to be curly brown but which he had bleached into a blonde hairstyle and which became a prominent hallmark used in cartoons. While comparisons such as these were obvious in the Dutch political landscape, they also had the effect of blurring the impact of the intended mirror Bukvić wanted her production to uphold. Even though reviewers spoke in terms of a production that confronted 'us' with our own perceptions (Janssens, 2018), the focus moved towards the usual suspects. Instead of the intended self-reflection, it allowed for safe and predictable accusations of others in Dutch society, thereby confining institutional racism to the corners of populist and xenophobe parties. One might argue that in this sense, the production let the politically correct left (and right) off the hook. Paradoxically, this rather confirmed the argument in the book *Hello White People*, an inspiration in the production, that the 'white, highly educated, intellectual and correct group' would be unaware of their own limited, racial perspective (Nzume, 2017a: 15–16; also Çankaya & Mepschen, 2019: 628–9).

On the choice of a black actor as Othello, reviewers were positive and agreed that it contributed to the focus of the production. Some commented on former casting decisions of Othello in the Netherlands and how these had employed 'white actors with blackface' (Hoogendoorn, 2018). This was done in a neutral manner, however, and one reviewer even placed this former approach in a wider international context:

> Although according to convention, Othello is played by a white actor with blackface, there have been many exceptions: in 1825 already the black actor Ira Aldridge staged a much-lauded Othello in London. (Freriks, 2018)

While one may argue about the popularity of Aldridge's performances in London, the convention of a white actor with blackface had been discredited long before the discussion on blackface had even started to emerge in the Netherlands. While many of the reviews discussed the racial discourse, most ignored the topic of blackface as such. Another reviewer compared this production to the 2001 production discussed before, which had also employed a black actor, and argued how both productions discussed similar topics:

> For those of us who are in the possession of a well-trained
> theatre memory, Bukvić directed the younger sister of Koos
> Terpstra's anarchistic *Othello* at the start of our new century,
> in which Eric von Sauers played a stand-up comedian loner,
> a foolish black clown in the circus of the devil Iago. In that
> production the racist cards were immediately on the table: 'I
> hate that *neger*.' (Zonneveld, 2018)

While the comments indicated an awareness of a burgeoning tradition of black actors for Othello, they also demonstrated that the 'well-trained theatre memory' was a fleeting concept. While the aforementioned opening line in the 2001 production might have resulted in a production that would initiate a discourse on racism or blackface, it did not materialise, as discussed in Section 4. Apart from the similarity of using a black actor, the productions of 2001 and 2018 were quite different. The resemblance hinted at in the comments was non-existent. When questioned on the comparison, Kolf stated that it illustrated a tendency in reviews on black actors:

> Reviewers in the Netherlands are all white. I have often
> talked about this with black colleagues and white reviewers
> look differently at black actors than at white actors. When a
> black actor performs well, they use words such as powerful,
> energetic and strong, those are the type of words you almost
> use for a black slave; when white actors perform well, they
> use words such as masterly, complex or subtle. I cannot take
> a reviewer such as Zonneveld seriously, because they don't
> take me seriously, they only look at me as a black actor and
> use all the stereotypes they have for us. (Kolf, 2020)

Although the production, its focus on the racial discourse and the presence of a black actor were applauded in reviews, the full potential and intent, aiming at highlighting institutional racism and blackface traditions both in the world of theatre and in the wider context of society, seemed not to be realised based on reception of the production. Moving beyond reviews, one should also pose the question to what extent actual audiences picked up on the production. While it would be hard for any audience member to ignore the basic core of the production and the introduction of the racial topic, there were some noticeable dissonances during performances. In part, these related to the race-based insults which were used in the production and which provoked laughter in the audience. Just as the 2003 and 2015 productions discussed earlier, this production used a translation commissioned specifically for it. Translator Esther Duysker argued that she focused on racial stereotyping. Like Willems, who translated the 2015 production, she referred to the festival of Saint Nicholas and Black Pete, for instance, and to deep-seated forms of institutional racism in Dutch society. To bring this across, she modernised the racial abuse in the play:

> Calling someone a Moor is for me the same as continually referring to someone as an 'African' or a '*neger*' today. You simply cannot use these words anymore. So, in my translation, I purposefully used as many painful synonyms for 'Moor' as possible to strengthen the production. For me, as a person [Duysker was confronted with racism herself on a regular basis in the Netherlands], it was not easy to use words such as '*neger*', and I noticed that the actors were also shocked by certain phrases. I understand this, but I think it brings the message across. (Duysker, 2018)

Although less brutally than Bouazza (2003) and Willems (2015) before her, Duysker did enhance racial stereotyping in her translation, using phrases such as 'silly ape' (Emilia) or 'a savage will always be a savage' (Lodovico). A topical translation of 'Moor' (2.1.220), in a conversation between Iago and Roderigo, was 'tropical mascot' (Duysker, 2017: 34). It was a direct reference to professional Dutch swimming champion Ranomi Kromowidjojo, who was born in the Netherlands to a Dutch mother and a Javanese Surinam father. She had won multiple gold medals during the 2008 and 2012 Olympics and was referred to as a 'tropical mascot' on Dutch television. In the 2018 production, however, the term was used as offensive racial stereotyping. Just as in the 2015 production, derogatory terms such as these also provoked unintended but muted laughter in the overwhelmingly white audience.

Even more laughter was heard during many of Iago's lines: while his evil intent was clear from the start, he used his many asides and one-liners to amuse the audience, who frequently burst out laughing. However, not everyone shared the same perception, and one out of five audience members the author spoke to after the staging of a production in Leeuwarden on 17 March 2018 and in Zwolle on 30 January 2020 remarked that they 'wondered why all these people were laughing. I could not laugh about it, there was nothing comical about it'. They were a minority in the audience, however, and for black persons in an overwhelmingly white audience, the laughter about Iago or racial abuse must have been even more uncomfortable. Gloria Wekker, the author of the study *White Innocence*, born in Surinam and having moved to the Netherlands shortly after, questioned the laughter during the performance from a personal perspective:

> Ninety-eight percent of the audience is white and that determines my personal perception. And the fact that they laugh about certain things that are quite painful to me creates an even greater distance between us ... The fact that audience members are laughing the moment someone uses a virulently racist term makes me think that they are amused and not painfully touched. (Wekker, 2018)

In response to Wekker's personal observations, a reviewer of *Volkskrant*, a Dutch left-wing newspaper somewhat comparable to *The Guardian*, replied that it was interesting to read how 'a black spectator [Gloria Wekker] experiences the explicit racism in the production – and particularly the fact that white audience members laugh about it occasionally' (Wensink, 2018). Further, Wensink argued that laughter did not imply agreement and might even force one to consider one's own unconscious racist attitude. While the reaction contained elements of condescension and in a sense might have arguably perpetuated institutional racism, the racial topic of *Othello* had turned into a matter of debate for the first time. In that sense, this production seemed not only to have reflected institutional racism of Dutch society, but also furthered the debate on this topic.

An interesting ambiguity in this debate was the seeming discrepancy between the generally favourable reception of the production of *Othello* versus the critical reception of *Hello White People* (Nzume, 2017a). The book, which formed the basis for this *Othello*, was derided as a poisonous product of identity politics by the very same newspapers which had hailed the discussion the *Othello* production provoked (Drayer, 2017). The moderate Christian newspaper *Trouw* accused Nzume of 'racist' attitudes (Ephimenco, 2017), leading to a discussion in the newspaper on the 'ever-continuing stream of white-hot reactions of colleagues on *Hello White People*' (Nourhussen, 2017). Nzume and Bukvić also appeared on discussion programmes, arguing how *Othello* and *Hello White People* addressed institutional racism and black-face traditions in Dutch society, a topic, they argued, largely ignored in the Netherlands (Bukvić, 2018a, 2020; Nzume, 2017b). While the ideas behind both the book and the production showed remarkable resemblances, the media and tone differed. The book set a direct, confrontational and purpose-fully accusatory tone that also clearly aimed to address the cultural and progressive elite. The production, on the other hand, presented an aestheti-cally pleasing, well-enacted product with a new approach to a well-known play on the Dutch stage. It also left room for criticism of Dutch theatre and racism, without the necessity of self-reflection. The derided message the book wanted to address was filtered through the aesthetics of the theatre and applauded. Politically correct indignation over others who discriminated took the place of critical self-reflection; whereas the theatre reviews allowed for a continuation of one's own moral superiority, one might argue that the book forced the reader directly and unavoidably into the role of the accused. The author herself identified the fierce criticism at the time as white fragility, the defensive attitude white people adopt who have had the luxury never to have been confronted with their skin colour (Nzume, 2017b). Some media outlets picked up on the relation with *Hello White People* and argued that the *Othello* by Bukvić cut deeply into this discussion on topics such as institutional racism and white privilege (Rijghard, 2018). Bukvić also pointed out the similarity: 'The questions she [Anousha Nzume] asks are the same questions I am asking in this *Othello*. We are not aware that we are living in a country where people are not treated equal. White people enjoy a historic privilege. If we would be aware of that, it might solve many problems' (Bukvić, 2018b).

As a particularly sensitive part of this debate, Bukvić also addressed one of the open wounds on the body of Dutch society and tradition – the discussion on Black Pete: 'Last year I was in Limburg, and I saw a Black Pete with all the caricatures. If my work can help in the debate, then I feel it matters' (Bukvić, 2018c). Although Black Pete as such was not mentioned in the production, Bukvić was openly supportive of the anti-Black Pete lobby. She posted online pictures of her with a T-shirt saying 'Black Pete is racism', and the programme notes of *Othello* and the introductory talks before the performances all referred to the debate. She also stated that she could 'never have made this production without the ongoing Black Pete debate, as it had been fuelled by that blind spot in Dutch society' (Bukvić, 2020). She drew a direct parallel between the inability to acknowledge the sensitivity of blackface in the popular tradition of Black Pete and the use of blackface on the Dutch stage in *Othello*:

> *Othello* is illustrative of how the Netherlands and the theatre sector deal with racism. They ignore it and turn it into a love tragedy. This beautiful play by Shakespeare, it is one on one relevant in our society, but no one does so. [They] are not capable of addressing the most important trouble spot in the Netherlands and discuss it in a play that actually deals with it. (Bukvić, 2017)

However, although the production was applauded and racism and the choice of a black actor figured prominently in reviews and became a topic of wider debate in the media, the reception was also ambivalent and, at times, defensive. Blackface and the tradition of Black Pete received hardly any attention at all. The debate on Black Pete, the ambivalent reactions and Othello's victimisation were topics Bukvić wanted to further address in the rerun in 2020, which is discussed next.

5.5 Epilogue: 2020 and Onwards

In 2020, *Othello* was given a rerun in Dutch theatres. By itself, the decision was an indication of the prominence of the production in the Dutch theatre world as reruns are rare. More significantly, instead of smaller auditoriums, the production was now staged in bigger auditoriums. It also contained some notable changes as compared to the previous time, particularly with present-day relevance for blackface in Dutch society and on stage, institutional racism and reduction of Othello's victimisation. The advertising for the production, through a one-minute teaser (accessible online: Nationale, 2020), indicated the more topical approach. The original teaser had limited itself to fragments with the actors and also included shots of two specific American activists: James Baldwin, as he spoke the words 'this really rather frightening world', and Nina Simone as she said, 'I insist upon not being one of your clowns' (Nationale, 2018). The 2020 trailer had added four references to topical racism in Dutch society: three references to Black Pete, including an anti-Black Pete activist being dragged forcefully away by police officers, and one reference to the 2019 incident of racially abused Dutch football player Ahmad Mendes Moreira discussed in Section 2. The relation between Dutch society and recent incidents involving racism and blackface was highlighted more so than before.

Another major change in the production was the ending. In the 2018 production, Othello was strangled by Iago, but in the 2020 production, Iago killed himself and Othello survived. This significant change had its roots in the rapidly changing and escalating context of the debate on institutional racism in Dutch society. After repeating the 2018 line 'Are you afraid of me?', the line 'From now on, we are going to do things differently' was added in the 2020 rerun. Next, Othello walked to the bed, which had been changed into a platform, climbed on top of it and raised his clenched fist, in a clear reference to the Black Power salute. The victimisation of 2018 was significantly reduced in this production, although Bukvić saw it as a process: 'Two years ago, I wanted to shake people awake with the raw reality. No matter how painful it was to see Othello being strangled on stage, I wanted to show people how institutional racism was strangling black people in this country' (Bukvić, 2020). In the intervening two years, racism and the debate on racism in the Netherlands had come out in the open more and also reached new heights, for example, in the ever-hardening and confrontational positions in the Black Pete debate or in the racial chants at the halted football match. For Bukvić, these developments meant that the changes aimed not only at reducing Othello's victimisation, as advocated earlier by Wekker (2018), but also at introducing an element of hope:

> Now, in 2020, that reality is so visible and so ugly, I felt it was time to end with hope and with empowerment, hence the fist. And of course, I am also referring to the global context, to *Django Unchained*, Colin Kaepernick, but also the Black Panthers and history. But I wanted to start the new decade of the twenty-first century with hope. Not only to tell white people something, but I also did not want black people to leave the auditorium with another stain on their soul. (Bukvić, 2020)

Kolf indicated how the fist, for him, was also a sign towards the 'white Dutch theatrical, the cultural world and their fear of me taking on this role' (Kolf, 2020). With this production, the debate on blackface in the theatrical world has inevitably come to the fore, entangled with debates on blackface and Black Pete as well. Whereas these topics were largely ignored in the fringe production of John Leerdam twenty years earlier, they now entered the heart of the Dutch theatre through one of its major companies. While it is always hard to gauge the impact of such a production, one may legitimately wonder whether *Othello* productions will still employ white actors in the foreseeable future, let alone make use of blackface. For Bukvić, it was not a matter of debate: 'Nobody is going to dare this anymore. Looking at the buzz surrounding our *Othello*, the media attention, I find it hard to believe that anyone in the next ten years is going to stage another *Othello* with a white actor' (Bukvić, 2020).

Only time will tell this, but that the debate on blackface and the racial discourse has finally entered the Dutch landscape and its theatre world is beyond any doubt. It is now a debate in which the *Othello* of Bukvić has played a significant part. In this study, the author has analysed the huge gap between *Othello* in the UK (and other anglophone countries) and the

Netherlands. Despite the proximity between the countries, the close ties by way of trade and culture, the overwhelming use of English in schools and the dominance of Shakespeare on stage, a wide gulf separated the *Othello* traditions. Through this study, the author aimed at providing a different perspective on blackface and race in a supposedly tolerant, Western country.

While the latest *Othello* ended on a hopeful note, in conclusion, the author wishes to invoke a sobering incident, one might even call it an anecdote were it not so painful and illustrative of the long way ahead. It happened at the kick-off of the *Othello* production, when the entire company, from the HR department to the canteen employees, came to watch and hear the director explain the themes of the production so that the entire theatre would know what it was about. The next day, as Bukvić entered the rehearsal room with the assistant director, she noticed the actor Kolf, who had arrived first, as he sat in a corner with his hands in his hair and tears in his eyes. Walking to the rehearsal table, Bukvić noted two big chocolate letters from the HR department, both with a depiction of Black Pete on them. Discussing the incident, she said:

> The depictions had these huge big mouths and red lips, golden earrings, the real ones. And him [Werner Kolf], sitting in the corner. It freaked me out. I thought, how on earth is this possible, after everything I [said] yesterday. Kill me. So, while you are making a production in the safety of your own company house, which is the biggest theatre company of the Netherlands, at the same time you are fighting the very systems which you are addressing in your production. I needed a vacation. (Bukvić, 2020)

References

Achiume, T. (2019). Cited in M. Corder, 'UN racism rapporteur criticizes Dutch burqa ban', *AP News*, 7 October.

Aerts, A. (2015). 'Hartverscheurende solo', *Dagblad de Limburger*, 10 July.

Akveld, J. (2015). 'Ivo's regie werkt gewoon', *Het Parool*, 5 May.

Alexander, C. M. S. & S. Wells, eds. (2000). *Shakespeare and Race*. Cambridge: Cambridge University Press.

Allen, T. W. (2012). *The Invention of the White Race* (2nd ed.). New York: Verso.

'Allochtonen zijn razend' (2000). *Contrast. Weekblad over de Multiculturele Samenleving*, 7: 3.

'Amsterdams museum doet "Gouden Eeuw" in de ban' (2019). *De Telegraaf*, 13 September.

Andriessen, I., E. Nievers & J. Dagevos (2012). *Op Achterstand. Discriminatie van Niet-Westerse Migranten op de Arbeidsmarkt*. Den Haag: Sociaal en Cultureel Planbureau.

Bahara, H. & N. Ezzeroili (2019). 'Zo werd het gewelddadig', *Volkskrant*, 16 November.

Barth, F. (1969). *Ethnic Groups and Boundaries. The Social Organization of Cultural Difference*. London: Allen & Unwin.

Bassett, K. (2000). 'OJ exploration is a bit of a trial', *The Telegraph*, 26 January.

Benedict, R. (1944). 'A note on Dutch behaviour'. In R. van Ginkel, ed., *Notities over Nederlanders. Antropologische Reflecties*. Meppel: Boom, 1997, 225–34.

Bentley, G. C. (1987). 'Ethnicity and practice'. *Comparative Studies in Society and History*, 29, 24–55.

Berkoff, S. (2015). Cited in J. Denham, 'Othello should not be a "no-go-zone" for white actors because of "political correctness fiends"', *Independent*, 16 June.

Billing, C. M. (2007). '"Othello was a white man": Review of *Othello* (directed by Luk Perceval for Münchner Kammerspiele) at the Royal Shakespeare Theatre, April 2006'. *Shakespeare*, 3:2, 189–99.

Blom, J. C. H. (1995). *Geschiedenis van de Joden in Nederland*. Amsterdam: Uitgeverij Balans.

Bobkova, H. (2003). 'Bijzonder rijke theatertaal', *Het Financieele Dagblad*, 22 February.

Boegman, C. (2015). 'Muzikale versie van Othello. Nieuwe weg van Servé Hermans en Michel Sluysmans', *De Telegraaf*, 26 June.

Bonilla-Silva, E. (2015). 'More than prejudice: Restatement, reflections, and new directions in critical race theory'. *Sociology of Race and Ethnicity*, 1:1, 75–89.

Booy, F. (2014). *Het Verhaal van Zwarte Piet: Geschiedenis en Betekenis*. Utrecht: Nederlands Centrum voor Volkscultuur en Immaterieel Erfgoed.

Boswinkel, H. (1971). 'Globe speelt Othello. Twee grote rollen zijn een beetje verkwist', *NRC Handelsblad*, 2 January.

Bots, P. (2001). 'Othello met te veel luim', *Het Parool*, 29 October.

Bouazza, H. (2001). *De Slachting In Parijs*. Amsterdam: Prometheus.

Bouazza, H. (2003). *William Shakespeare. Othello. Vertaald en van Commentaar Voorzien door Hafid Bouazza*. Amsterdam: Prometheus.

Bovenkerk, F. (1995). *Discrimination against Migrant Workers and Ethnic Minorities in Access to Employment in the Netherlands*. Geneva: International Labour Office.

Boyle, M. S. (2012). 'Review of Shakespeare's *Othello* (directed by Thomas Ostermeier), Schaubühne am Lehnitzer Platz, Berlin, 8 February 2011', *Shakespeare*, 8:1, 83–6.

Brans, H. (2018). 'Vreemde vrucht: Othello moet hangen', *Dagblad van het Noorden*, 19 March.

Brienen, R. P. (2014). 'Types and stereotypes: Zwarte Piet and his early modern sources'. In P. Essed & I. Hoving, eds., *Dutch Racism*. Amsterdam/New York: Rodopi, 179–200.

Buddingh, H. (2017). *De Geschiedenis van Suriname*. Amsterdam: Uitgeverij Rainbow.

Buijs, M. (1988). 'Slotvoorstelling van toneelgroep Globe werkt Othello drama keurig af', *Volkskrant*, 5 April.

Buijs, M. (1996). 'Othello is een eendimensionale vertoning', *Volkskrant*, 9 April.

Buijs, M. (2001). 'Tragedie legt het af tegen kolder', *Volkskrant*, 30 October.

Bukvić, D. (2017). Interviewed by H. Wensink, 'Ik heb schijt aan hoe het heurt', *Volkskrant*, 16 December.

Bukvić, D. (2018a). Interviewed by S. Kooke, 'Waanzinning goed én zwart', *Trouw*, 1 February.

Bukvić, D. (2018b). Cited in R. Rijghard, 'Huidskleur kun je niet spelen', *NRC Handelsblad*, 31 January.

Bukvić, D. (2018c). Interviewed by R. van Heuven, 'Daria Bukviç: "Ik preek niet, ik bied een perspectief"', *Robbert van Heuven, Kritiek en Reflectie*. Accessed on 2 March 2020. www.robbertvanheuven.nl/?p=2150

Bukvić, D. (2020). Interview by Coen Heijes, Café Czaar, Amsterdam, 4 February.

Çankaya, S. & P. Mepschen (2019). 'Facing racism: Discomfort, innocence and the liberal peripheralisation of race in the Netherlands'. *Social Anthropology/Anthropologie Sociale*, 27:4, 626–40.

Carmiggelt, S. (1951). 'Ko van Dijk's Othello oogstte geestdrift in Rotterdam', *Het Parool*, 17 May.

Cooper, M. (2015). 'An "Otello" without blackface highlights an enduring tradition in opera', *New York Times*, 17 September.

Cozijnsen, E., S. Kromhout & L. Wittkämper (2019). *Discriminatie op de Amsterdamse Woningmarkt. Praktijktesten in de Particuliere Huursector.* Amsterdam: RIGO.

Day, M, E. Klooster & S. Koçak (2016). *Wat is er Bekend over Discriminatie van Mbostudenten bij Toegang tot de Stagemarkt?* Utrecht: Kennisplatform Integratie & Samenleving.

De Gids van Drenthe, Het Nationale Park van Drenthe, Summer 2013: 11. Accessed on 2 March 2020. www.hetnationaleparkvandrenthe.nl/ uploads/De%20Gids%20zomereditie%20def%2020130619.pdf

de Groot, J. H. (1977). 'Zadeks Othello: de spetters vlogen er aan alle kanten af', *Het Vrije Volk*, 16 May.

de Jong, A. (2003a). 'Kiezen op elkaar en voorwaarts. Hans Kesting over Othello', *NRC Handelsblad*, 1 February.

de Jong, A. (2003b). 'Theater. Ook Desdemona is schuldig', Opzij, 1 March.

de Jong, S. (2018). 'Zwarte Othello in een witte wereld', *De Gooi- en Eemlander*, 5 February.

de Jong, W., Masson, K. & Steijlen, F. (1997). *Hoe Doe je je Ding? Antilliaanse Jongeren en Criminaliteit.* Delft: Eburon.

de Lange, D. (1971). 'Stuk laat alle mogelijkheden open. Regie-opvatting Othello te ruim. Fantasie kan platvloers worden', *Volkskrant*, 4 January.

de Lange, D. (1977). 'Krachtpatserij van Zadek. Overweldigende Othello overtuigt elk ogenblijk', *Volkskrant*, 16 May.

de Ruiter, E. (1988). 'Onevenwichtige Othello als afscheid Globe', *Telegraaf*, 5 April.

de Vries, S. de (1989). 'Othello in Diever: helder als glas', *Leeuwarder Courant*, 6 July.

'Den Bosch-Excelsior stilgelegd wegens racisme: "Boos en teleurgesteld dat dit gebeurt"', *Het Parool*, 17 November 2019.

Devens, T. (2015). 'Een vermakelijk avondje uit met Othello', *Theaterkrant*, 26 June.

DiAngelo, R. J. (2018). *White Fragility: Why It's So Hard for White People to Talk about Racism*. Boston: Beacon Press.

Doesburg, J. (2020). Interview by Coen Heijes, The Hague, 28 February.

Drayer, E. (2017). 'Hallo Witte Mensen is te zeer product uit het giffabriekje identiteitspolitiek', *Volkskrant*, 28 April.

Dubbelman, J. E. & J. Tanja (1987). *Vreemd Gespuis*. Amsterdam: Ambo.

Duysker, E. (2017). *Othello. Definitieve Speelversie*. Den Haag: Het Nationale Theater.

Duysker, E. (2018). Interviewed by V. Kouters, 'Theater', *Volkskrant*, 5 January 2018.

Duyvendak, J. W. & L. Veldboer (2001). *Meeting Point Nederland. Over Samenlevingsopbouw, Multiculturaliteit en Sociale Cohesie*. Amsterdam: Uitgeverij Boom.

Editorial, 'Zwarte Piet blijft grotendeels zwart in Limburg', *1Limburg*, 20 September 2019.

Ellemers, J. E. & R. E. F. Vaillant (1985). *Indische Nederlanders en Gerepatrieerden*. Muiderberg: Coutinho.

Elmecky, K. (2003). Interviewed by W. Takken, 'Wij zijn niet de negertjes in de Nes. Khaldoun Elmecky is de nieuwe directeur van Cosmictheater', *NRC Handelsblad*, 27 March.

Ephimenco, S. (2017). 'Het zwarte privilege van Anousha Nzume', *Trouw*, 2 May.

Essed, P. (1984). *Alledaags Racisme*. Amsterdam: Feministische Uitgeverij Sara.

Essed, P. & I. Hoving, eds. (2014). *Dutch Racism*. Amsterdam/New York: Rodopi.

Fernhout, R. (2003). Interviewed by E. Kleuver, 'Knokken voor elke millimeter', *De Telegraaf*, 31 January.

Fields, K. E. & B. J. Fields (2012). *Racecraft: The Soul of Inequality in American Life*. London: Verso.

Freriks, K. (1997). 'Monumentale Othello van Franz Marijnen in Brussel en house-versie in Den Haag', *NRC Handelsblad*, 4 April.

Freriks, K. (2001). 'Van luim naar ernst en terug in Terpstra's Othello', *NRC Handelsblad*, 30 October.

Freriks, K. (2006). 'Zaal medeplichtig aan Othello's moord', *NRC Handelsblad*, 30 October.

Freriks, K. (2013). 'Iago zelf verliefd in Dieverse Othello', *NRC Handelsblad*, 13 August.

Freriks, K. (2015). 'Meedogenloze Othello in Valkenburg', *NRC Handelsblad*, 8 July.

Freriks, K. (2018). 'Niemand kan wegkijken van het blank racisme', *NRC. NEXT*, 5 February.

Gardner, L. (1998). 'OJ/Othello', *The Guardian*, 12 August.

Geerlings, E. (1996). 'Een Othello van de straat', *Algemeen Dagblad*, 9 April.

Gielkens, D. & F. Wegkamp (2019). Onderzoeksrapport: *Discriminatie op de Utrechtse Woningmarkt*. Amsterdam: Academie van de Stad.

Griffioen, P. & R. Zeller (2011). *Jodenvervolging in Nederland, Frankrijk en België 1940–1945: Overeenkomsten, Verschillen, Oorzaken*. Amsterdam: Uitgeverij Boom.

Gybels, S. (2014). 'Zwarte Piet in Maastricht blijft zwart', *1Limburg*, 23 September.

Hadfield, A., ed. (2003). *A Routledge Literary Sourcebook on William Shakespeare's Othello*. London/New York: Routledge.

Hankey, J. (2005). *Shakespeare in Production. Othello. Second Edition*. Cambridge: Cambridge University Press.

Hartering, W. (1964). 'Ko van Dijk en Paul Steenbergen. Grote acteurs voor het eerst samen op toneel', *De Telegraaf*, 22 June.

Heddema, R. (1980). 'Nijinsky brengt een Othello voor ingewijden', *Volkskrant*, 27 September.

Heijer, J. (1980). 'Een Othello met oosterse sereniteit bij Nijinsky', *NRC Handelsblad*, 3 October.

Heijes, C. (2001). *Met Andere Ogen. Wonen en Werken in Multicultureel Nederland. Vierentwintig verhalen*. Den Haag: Sdu.

Heijes, C. (2003). 'Yu'i Korsou in Nederland. Geschiedenis en beeldvorming'. In R. M. Allen, C. Heijes & V. Marcha, eds.,*Emancipatie & Acceptatie. Curaçao en Curaçaoënaars. Beeldvorming en Identiteit Honderdveertig Jaar na de Slavernij*. Amsterdam: SWP, 91–110.

Heijes, C. (2004). *Het Stereotype Voorbij. Een Studie naar Onbegrip, Beeldvorming en Samenwerking*. Amsterdam: SWP.

Hellmann, N. (1993). 'Pierre Bokma speelt intrigant Iago meesterlijk. Verdriet en destructie in Othello hartverscheurend', *NRC Handelsblad*, 23 April.

Hellmann, N. (1998). 'Frank Sheppard spelt een prachtige Othello-figuur', *NRC Handelsblad*, 6 April.

Helsloot, J. (2008). 'De ambivalente boodschap van de eerste 'Zwarte Piet' (1850)'. In E. Doelman & J. Helsloot, eds.,*De Kleine Olympus: Over Enkele Figuren uit de Alledaagse Mythologie*. Amsterdam: Koninklijke Nederlandse Academie van Wetenschappen, 93–117.

Hendrikx, A. (2015). 'Zwarte Piet is toch gewoon zwart in Maastricht', *1Limburg*, 14 November.

Hermans, S. (2015a). Interviewed by V. Kouters, 'Exotisch snoepje', *Volkskrant*, 20 March.

Hermans, S. (2015b). Interviewed by E. Korsten, 'Shakespeares klassieker *Othello* met muziek van Verdi. Het scheermes van het eigen ongeloof', *Scènes*, June/July: 42–3.

Heyn Jr, J. (1951). 'Rotterdamse Othello onder de maat', *De Telegraaf*, 17 May.

'Hij komt, hij komt' & 'Pakjesavond goud waard' (2018). *De Telegraaf*, 17 November, 1–3.

Hofstra, J. W. (1951). 'Prachtige Othello bij Rotterdams Toneel. Shakespeare in de beste traditie', *Volkskrant*, 17 September.

Hoogendoorn, M. (2018). 'Othello en de vele gezichten van racisme', *Nederlands Dagblad*, 16 February.

Hoogmartens, L. (2001). Interviewed by M. van der Laan, 'Terpstra laat acteurs struikelen en zoeken', *Dagblad van het Noorden*, 23 October.

Hoving, I. (2014). 'Dutch postcolonialism, multiculturalism and national identity: society, theory, literature'. In D. Göttsche & A. Dunker, eds., *(Post-) Colonialism across Europe: Transcultural History and National Memory*. Bielefeld: Aisthesis Verlag, 57–86.

Inspectie van het Onderwijs (2020). *Rapport de Staat van het Onderwijs 2020*. Den Haag: Ministerie van Onderwijs, Cultuur en Wetenschap.

Iyengar, S. (2002). 'White faces, blackface. The production of "Race" in *Othello*', in P. C. Kolin, ed. *Othello. New Critical Essays*. London/ New York: Routledge, 103–31.

Jaarrapport Integratie (2007 et seq.). Den Haag: Centraal Bureau voor de Statistiek.

Jackson Sr, J. L. (2020). 'Personal Letter to Prime Minister Mark Rutte', in *De Kanttekening*, 18 June 2020. Accessed on 22 July 2020. https:// dekanttekening.nl/samenleving/afro-amerikaanse-dominee-jesse-jackson-schrijft-rutte-brief-over-zwarte-piet/.

Jansen, H. (2013). 'Zwarte Pieten met Othello', *William.*, Summer 2: 18.

Janssen, H. (2003). 'Van Hove is terug met bloedstollende Othello. Hans Kesting groeit uit tot gekweld oermens', *Volkskrant*, 3 February.

Janssen, H. (2013). 'Othello', *Volkskrant*, 13 August.

Janssen, H. (2018). 'Othello. Theaterrecensie', *Volkskrant*, 5 February.

Janssens, S. (2018). 'Othello is zwart, en dat doet er wel degelijk toe', *Het Parool*, 6 February.

Jarrett-Macauley, D., ed. (2017). *Shakespeare, Race and Performance*. London/New York: Routledge.

Jurriëns, R. (2001). 'Twee culturen maken je erg complex', in C.Heijes, ed., *Met Andere Ogen. Wonen en Werken in Multicultureel Nederland*. The Hague: SdU, 46–51.

Kalkman, N. (2020). 'Moorkop afgedankt: "Opportunisme van winkelketens"', *De Telegraaf*, 6 February.

Kalverboer, M. (2016a). Cited in M. van Ast, 'Kinderombudsman: Zwarte Piet in strijd met kinderrechten', *Algemeen Dagblad*, 30 September.

Kalverboer, M. (2016b). 'Kinderombudsman doet aangifte na doodsbedreigingen', *Algemeen Dagblad*, 3 October.

Kennedy, D. (1996). *Looking at Shakespeare. A Visual History of Twentieth-Century Performance*. Cambridge: Cambridge University Press.

Kesting, H. (2003). Interviewed by A. de Jong, 'Kiezen op elkaar en voorwaarts. Hans Kesting over Othello', *NRC Handelsblad*, 1 February.

Kleuver, E. (2013). 'Othello duikt weer op in Diever', *De Telegraaf*, 8 August.

Kloosterman, R. (2018). *Opvattingen over Vluchtelingen in Nederland*. Den Haag: Centraal Bureau voor de Statistiek.

Kolf, W. (2020). Interview by Coen Heijes, Café Czaar, Amsterdam, 4 February.

Kolin, P. C., ed. (2002). *Othello. New Critical Essays*. London/New York: Routledge.

Koning, E. (2018). 'Zwarte Piet, een blackfacepersonage: Een eeuw aan blackfacevermaak in Nederland'. *Tijdschrift voor Geschiedenis*, 131:4, 551–75.

Koot, W. (1979). *Emigratie op de Nederlandse Antillen. Een Sociaal-Wetenschappelijk Onderzoek naar Omvang en Achtergronden van de*

Emigratie, in het Bijzonder op Aruba en Curaçao. Amsterdam: Universiteit van Amsterdam.

Kwei-Armah, K. (2004). 'My problem with the Moor', *The Guardian*, 7 April.

Langen, F. (2001). 'Othello raakt bij NNT uit balans', *Dagblad van het Noorden*, 29 October.

Leerdam, J. (1998a). Interviewed by A. de Jong, 'Leerdam smeedt O. J. Simpson en Othello samen. Een complexe man op zoek naar vaderliefde', *NRC Handelsblad*, 3 April.

Leerdam, J. (1998b). Cited in J. van Lingen, 'Theater', *Het Parool*, 3 September.

Leerdam, J. (1998c). Interviewed by R. Gerrits, 'Zonder verschillen is er ook geen melodie', *Volkskrant*, 4 August.

Loomba, A. (2008). 'Shakespeare and the possibilities of postcolonial performance'. In B. Hodgdon & W. B. Worthen, eds., *A Companion to Shakespeare and Performance*. Oxford: Wiley-Blackwell, 121–37.

Lucassen, J. & R. Penninx (1999). *Nieuwkomers, Nakomelingen, Nederlanders. Immigranten in Nederland 1550–1993*. Amsterdam: Het Spinhuis.

Massai, S. (2018). 'Directing the classics'. In S. Bennett & S. Massai, eds.,*Ivo van Hove. From Shakespeare to David Bowie*. London: Methuen Drama, Bloomsbury, 19–28.

McMillan, J. (1998). 'Is OJ really an Othello for the nineties?', *The Scotsman*, 10 August.

Michiel de Ruyter. Director R. Reiné. Film. Farmhouse Film & TV, 2015.

Michman, J., H. Beem & D. Michman (1992). *Pinkas. Geschiedenis van de Joodse Gemeenschap in Nederland*. Amsterdam: Joods Historisch Museum.

Monitor Racisme, Antisemitisme en Extreem Rechts (1997 et seq.). Amsterdam: Anne Frank Stichting.

Moore, B. (1997). *Victims & Survivors. The Nazi Persecution of the Jews in the Netherlands 1940–1945*. New York: Arnold.

Moose minirecensies (2001). *Othello NNT*. Accessed on 11 February 2020. www.moose.nl/minirecensies/othello-noord-nederlands-toneel/index.html

Nationale Theater (2018). *Teaser of the Othello Productions of 2018*, company website. Accessed on 14 February 2020. www.hnt.nl/pQOOvTP/othello

Nationale Theater (2020). *Teaser of the Othello Productions of 2020*, company website. Accessed on 14 February 2020. www.hnt.nl/voorstellingen/3166/Het_Nationale_Theater/Othello

Nederkoorn, E. (2013). 'Othello is geen Drent', *Leeuwarder Courant*, 8 August.

Nederpelt, R. (2003). 'Van Hove maakt indrukwekkende Othello', *Eindhovens Dagblad*, 22 March.

Neill, M. (2006). *William Shakespeare. Othello, the Moor of Venice*. Oxford: Oxford University Press.

Nieborg, J. (2013a). Interviewed by E. Nederkoorn, 'Othello is geen Drenth', *Leeuwarder Courant*, 8 August.

Nieborg, J. (2013b). *Shakespeare. Othello*. Winsum: Grobein.

Nieuwerf, M. (2018). Interviewed by R. Rijghard, 'Het racisme in Othello is onmiskenbaar', *NRC Handelsblad*, 1 February.

Nightingale, B. (1998). 'OJ comes to Edinburgh', *The Times*, 12 August.

Nourhussen, S. (2017). 'Noem me mevrouw Nourhussen, Sylvain', *Trouw*, 4 May.

Nzume, A. (2017a). *Hallo Witte Mensen*. Amsterdam: Amsterdam University Press.

Nzume, A. (2017b). Interviewed by M. de Cocq, 'Ik wist: dat gaat er niet in als koek', *Het Parool*, 24 April.

Omi, M. & H. Winant (2014). *Racial Formation in the United States* (3rd ed.). New York: Routledge.

Oostindie, G. (2002). Interviewed by C. Heijes, *Het Stereotype Voorbij. Een Studie naar Onbegrip, Beeldvorming en Samenwerking*. Amsterdam: SWP 234.

Oranje, H. (2003). 'Jong publiek uit zijn dak voor Othello', *Trouw*, 3 February.

'Othello bij het Rotterdams Toneel' (1951). *De Tijd: Godsdienstig-Staatkundig Dagblad*, 17 September.

'Othello, William Shakespeare' (2013). *William.*, 2, Summer.

Poliakov, L. (1975). *The History of Anti-Semitism, Volume III: From Voltaire to Wagner*. London: Routledge and Kegan Paul.

Potter, L. (2002). *Shakespeare in Performance. Othello*. Manchester: Manchester University Press.

Prins, B. (2004). *Voorbij de Onschuld. Het Debat over de Multiculturele Samenleving*. Amsterdam: Uitgeverij van Gennep.

Prinssen, M. (2003). 'Van toeschouwer tot ooggetuige bij Toneelgroep Amsterdam. Scherpe Othello van Hans Kesting', *Utrechts Nieuwsblad*, 3 February 2003.

Program Notes Othello (1980). Amsterdam: Nijinsky.

Prop, J. (2015). 'Fraaie uitvoering omarmd door unieke locatie', *Dagblad de Limburger*, 29 June.

Publieksreacties Toneelgroep Maastricht (2019). Accessed on 25 May 2019. www.toneelgroepmaastricht.nl/voorstelling/othello/extra/publieksreacties

Quarshie, H. (1999). *Second Thoughts about Othello. Occasional Paper No. 7*, Chipping Camden: International Shakespeare Association.

Rapport Inspectie SZW Mystery Calling-Onderzoek Arbeidsmarktdiscriminatie (2019). Den Haag: Inspectie Sociale Zaken en Werkgelegenheid.

Rapportage Minderheden (1993 *et seq.*). Den Haag: Sociaal en Cultureel Planbureau.

Rijghard, R. (2018). 'Huidskleur kun je niet spelen', *NRC Handelsblad*, 31 January.

Rings, P. (2013). 'Othello's achterdocht in Drenthe', *Theaterkrant*, 12 August.

Römer, T. (2006). Interviewed by W. Takken, 'Bovenal een verliefde soldaat. Acteur Thijs Römer over zijn vertolking van Othello', *NRC Handelsblad*, 27 October.

Roodnat, J. (1998). 'O. J. en de opvolging', *NRC Handelsblad*, 17 April.

Rozett, M. T. (1991). 'Talking back to Shakespeare. Student-reader responses to *Othello*'. In V. M. Vaughan & K. Cartwright, eds., *Othello. New Perspectives*. London/Toronto: Associated University Presses, 256–70.

Ruiten, A. (1980). 'Othello's jaloezie in beeld', *Trouw*, 30 September.

Rutte, M. (2019). Cited in H. Keultjes, 'Rutte: "Gouden Eeuw juist prachtige term, wat een onzin, pff"', *Algemeen Dagblad*, 13 September.

Rutte, M. (2020). In A. van Eijsden, 'Mark Rutte: Zwarte Piet is "geen racisme"', *Nederlands Dagblad*, 6 June 2020.

Schaap, W. (1997). 'Othello', *Algemeen Dagblad*, 5 April.

Schaap, W. (2001). 'Zwarte comedy uut Grunning', *Algemeen Dagblad*, 25 October.

Schaap, W. (2015). 'Discussie over kleur moet ook in schouwburg woeden', *Cultuurpers*, 8 May. Accessed on 11 February 2020. https://culture elpersbureau.nl/2015/05/discussie-kleur-moet-ook-schouwburgen-woeden/

Schenkman, J. (1850). *Sint Nikolaas en zijn Knecht*. Amsterdam: G. Theod. Bom.

Scholten, H. (1980). 'Othello', *Nieuwsblad van het Noorden*, 22 December.

Schouten, M. (1993). 'Een klassiek Othello voor scholieren', *Volkskrant*, 23 April.

Schuhmacher, P. (1987). *De Minderheden. 700,000 Migranten Minder Gelijk*. Amsterdam: Uitgeverij van Gennep.

Shepherd, V. (2017). 'UWI professor still receives Dutch hate mail, four years after criticising Dutch tradition', *Jamaica Observer*, 15 December.

Simons, J. (1993). Interviewed by T. Ruiter, 'Eerst zwart, dan bruin, dan wit, dan … ', *Volkskrant*, 21 May.

Smith, M. (2003). 'Bij Ivo van Hove is Othello geen Moor maar een Marokkaan. Tragedie met een ondertoon van vreemdelingenhaat', *Utrechts Nieuwsblad*, 26 February.

Spierdijk, J. (1971). 'Nieuwjaarspremière van Othello onacceptabele voorstelling', *De Telegraaf*, 4 January.

Sterke, W. (2020). Interview by Coen Heijes, Groningen, 12 March.

Stone, J. (1996). 'Ethnicity'. In A. Kuper & J. Kuper, eds., *The Social Science Encyclopedia. Second Edition*. London: Routledge, 260–3.

Straatman, T. (1988). 'Mooie vondsten in een tweeslachtige Othello bij Globe', *NRC Handelsblad*, 5 April.

Strien, P. (2001). 'Melige Othello loopt leeg', *Dagblad van het Noorden*, 29 October.

Takken, W. (2003a). 'Het multiculturele drama', *NRC Handelsblad*, 28 February.

Takken, W. (2003b). 'Arabische *Othello* als kippige Colin Powell', *NRC Handelsblad*, 3 February.

ten Bruggencate, C. (2003). 'Kanttekeningen van een vrouwelijke toneelspeler bij de euforsiche ontvangst van een Othello-enscenering in 2003', *NRC Handelsblad*, 14 February.

ter Horst-Rep, W. (1989). Interviewed by S. de Vries, 'Othello in Diever: helder als glas', *Leeuwarder Courant*, 6 July.

Terdu, T. (2013). 'Belevingsverslag Othello', *Thirʒa CKV*, 9 September.

Terpstra, K. (2001a). Interviewed by T. van den Bergh, 'Toneel: tegen de theaterpolitie', *Elseviers Weekblad*, 3 November.

Terpstra, K. (2001b). Interviewed by W. Schaap, 'Zwarte comedy uut Grunning', *Algemeen Dagblad*, 25 October.

Tesser, P. T. M., J. G. F. Merens & C. S. van Praag (1999). *Rapportage Minderheden*. Den Haag: Sociaal Cultureel Planbureau.

Thijssen, L., M. Coenders & B. Lancee (2018). 'Etnische discriminatie op de Nederlandse arbeidsmarkt Verschillen tussen etnische groepen en de rol van beschikbare informatie over sollicitanten', *Mens en Maatschappij*, 94.2: 141–76.

Thompson, A., ed. (2006). *Colorblind Casting. New Perspectives on Race and Performance*. London/New York: Routledge.

Thompson, A. (2016). Introduction. In E. A. J. Honigmann, ed., *The Arden Shakespeare. Othello*. London: Bloomsbury, 1–116.

'Tientallen demonstranten bij première Michiel de Ruyter' (2015). *Volkskrant*, 26 January.

Tinnemans, W. (1994). *Een Gouden Armband. Een Geschiedenis van Mediterrane Immigranten in Nederland 1954–1994*. Utrecht: Nederlands Centrum Buitenlanders.

United Nations (1965). *International Convention on the Elimination of All Forms of Racial Discrimination*, New York, 21 December.

Van Andel, C. P. (1983). *Jodenhaat en Jodenangst: Over Meer dan Twintig Eeuwen AntiSemitisme*. Amsterdam: Protestantse Stichting Lectuurvoorlichting ism de Anne Frank Stichting.

Van Arkel, D. (1984). 'De Groei van het anti-Joodse stereotype: een poging tot een hypothetisch deductieve werkwijze in historisch onderzoek'. *Tijdschrift voor Sociale Geschiedenis*, 10, 34–70.

Van de Harst, H.(1988). 'Afscheidsstuk Globe visueel fraai maar oneven-wichtig', *Trouw*, 27 April.

Van den Bergh, H. (1977). 'Duitse Othello. Volksverlakkerij', *Parool*, May 16.

Van der Heijden, C. (2017). 'Vijftien jaar na de moord op Pim Fortuyn. Dat zeg je niet!', *De Groene Amsterdammer*, 3 May.

Van der Jagt, M. (1998). 'O. J. is Othello, negerboefje en meer', *Volkskrant*, 6 April.

Van der Kooi, S. (2018). 'Belangrijke thema's, maar te weinig nuance in Othello', *Trouw*, 5 February.

Van der Laan, M. (2001). 'Terpstra laat acteurs struikelen en zoeken', *Dagblad van het Noorden*, 23 October.

Van der Noll, J. (2016). 'Dutch racism', *Ethnic and Racial Studies*, 39:3, 533–4.

Van Dijk, F. (1951). 'Ko van Dijk's Othello oogstte geestdrift in Rotterdam', *Het Parool*, 17 May.

Van Ginkel, R. (1997). *Notities over Nederlanders. Antropologische Reflecties*, Meppel: Boom.

Van Hensbergen, L. (1970). 'Othello als botsing van twee culturen', *NRC Handelsblad*, 31 December.

Van Hove, I. (2003). Interviewed by L. van Voorst, 'Doorleefde vertaling basis voor snijdende Othello', *De Stentor/Deventer Dagblad*, 5 March.

Van Hove, I. (2012). Interviewed by M. Arian, 'Ivo van Hove over zijn Feeks, Othello en Romeinse Tragedies', *De Groene Amsterdammer*, 23 August: 46–9.

Van Hulst, H. (1997). *Morgen Bloeit het Diabaas. De Antilliaanse Volksklasse in de Nederlandse Samenleving*. Amsterdam: Het Spinhuis.

Van Ruiten, J. (2013). 'Vieze spelletjes in Diever', *Dagblad van het Noorden*, 12 August.

Van Sauers, E. (2001). Interviewed by M. van der Laan, 'Terpstra laat acteurs struikelen en zoeken', *Dagblad van het Noorden*, 23 October.

Van Uffelen, R. (1993). Interviewed by T. Ruiter, 'Eerst zwart, dan bruin, dan wit, dan . . . ', *Volkskrant*, 21 May.

Vanvugt, E. (2011). *Nieuw Zwartboek van Nederland Overzee. Wat Iedere Nederlander Moet Weten*. Amsterdam: Aspekt.

Vaughan, V. M. (1994). *Othello. A Contextual History*. Cambridge: Cambridge University Press.

Vaughan, V. M. & K. Cartwright, eds. (1991). *Othello. New Perspectives*. London/Toronto: Associated University Presses.

Veenman, J. (1999). *Participatie en Perspectief. Verleden en Toekomst van Etnische Minderheden in Nederland*. Houten: Bohn, Stafleu van Loghum.

Veraart, K. (2006). 'Innemende Othello van Doesburg', *Volkskrant*, 30 October.

Veraart, K. (2015). 'De Sutters Othello is ontroerend in zijn naïviteit en Michaël Pas' Iago is geestig en sluw in deze nieuwe Shakespearevertaling', *Volkskrant*, 29 June.

Verheul, J. (2009). '"How could this have happened in Holland?" American perceptions of Dutch multiculturalism after 9/11'. In D. Rubin & J., Verheul, eds., *American Multiculturalism after 9/11: Transatlantic Perspectives*. Amsterdam: Amsterdam University Press, 191–205.

Vervoort, W. (2001). 'Een overdadig opgeleukte Othello van het NNT', *Leeuwarder Courant*, 18 October.

Verwoerd, J. (2020). Cited in M. van Gruijthuijsen, 'Jurgen (47) sluit bakkerij vanwege bedreigingen om moorkop: "Ik wil geen negerkop verkopen"', *Algemeen Dagblad*, 6 February.

Vital, D. (1999). *A People Apart. A Political History of the Jews in Europe 1789–1939*. Oxford: Oxford University Press.

Vroom, N. (1980). 'Bart Kiene opvallende Othello', *De Waarheid*, 30 September.

Wekker, G. (2016). *White Innocence. Paradoxes of Colonialism and Race*. Durham/London: Duke University Press.

Wekker, G. (2018). Interviewed by M. Lems, 'Naar Othello met Gloria Wekker', *Theatermaker*, 21 January.

Wells, S. (2015). Cited in G. Snow, 'Stanley Wells: "White actors should be allowed to play Othello"'. *The Stage*, 8 May.

Wensink, H. (2018). 'Wekker had liever een krachtige Othello gezien, een held die zegeviert, maar dat is dramatisch niet interessant', *Volkskrant*, 13 April.

Wet Inburgering Nieuwkomers (1998). Den Haag:Staatsblad 261.

Wheatcroft, D. (1997). 'Sorry, sweetheart, but whites need not apply', *Sunday Telegraph*, 21 September.

Willems, J. (2015). *William Shakespeare. Othello. Vrije vertaling van Jibbe Willems*. Amsterdam: De Nieuwe Toneelbibliotheek.

Winterman, P. (2020). 'Mensen stappen niet zomaar op een racist af', *Dagblad van het Noorden*, 10 February.

Zeeman, M. (1988). 'Globe vertelt verhaaltje voor het slapen gaan', *Leeuwarder Courant*, 29 April.

Zonneveld, L. (1996). 'Treurig COC-toneel met rode tepels', *De Groene Amsterdammer*, 17 April.

Zonneveld, L. (2003). 'De generaal, de stoeipoes en de schizofreen: *Othello*', *Etcetera*, 86, 57–8.

Zonneveld, L. (2012). 'Negen jaar verder. Othello', *De Groene Amsterdammer*, 13 September.

Zonneveld, L. (2018). 'Toneel. Othello', *De Groene Amsterdammer*, 15 February.

Cambridge Elements ≡

Shakespeare Performance

W. B. Worthen
Barnard College

W. B. Worthen is Alice Brady Pels Professor in the Arts, and Chair of the Theatre Department at Barnard College. He is also co-chair of the Ph.D. Program in Theatre at Columbia University, where he is Professor of English and Comparative Literature.

About the Series

Shakespeare Performance is a dynamic collection in a field that is both always emerging and always evanescent. Responding to the global range of Shakespeare performance today, the series launches provocative, urgent criticism for researchers, graduate students and practitioners. Publishing scholarship with a direct bearing on the contemporary contexts of Shakespeare performance, it considers specific performances, material and social practices, ideological and cultural frameworks, emerging and significant artists and performance histories.

Cambridge Elements ☰

Shakespeare Performance

Printed in the United States
By Bookmasters